The Poolbeg Book of
IRISH
HERALDRY

MICHEÁL Ó COMÁIN

POOLBEG

A Paperback Original
First published 1991 by Poolbeg Press Ltd
Knocksedan House,
Swords, Co Dublin, Ireland

© Micheál Ó Comáin 1991

ISBN 1 85371 126 8

Cover design by Pomphrey Associates
Original illustrations by Hereward King
Set by Richard Parfrey in ITC Stone 10/13
Printed by The Guernsey Press Company Ltd,
Vale, Guernsey, Channel Islands

Contents

For Moirita

Author's Preface

Should my knowledge of heraldry ever equal my enthusiasm for it I will doubtless be a notable scholar. In the meantime I must enter a plea of mitigation for having written even a short book. It is that no one else has taken the trouble. I say so with some gratitude, for had a novices' book of Irish heraldry been available to me I would have been denied a good deal of pleasure researching this one.

Even the otherwise exact writers of various useful primers, and those of some more advanced works, have been content to regard Irish armory as something subsidiary to that of England. I mean no unkindness by pointing out that the majority of them have been Englishmen and naturally more concerned with their own heraldic tradition than with ours. But an Irish heraldic tradition does exist, and one which I hope to show as distinctive in many ways. Irish armory lacks neither academic expertise nor its enthusiasts, but the lack of a previous guide to it is remarkable in a country which takes such a well-known pride in every aspect of its cultural heritage.

I intend that this short book should provide an introduction to heraldry as a whole and to Irish heraldry in particular. Perhaps it will prompt readers to take up some of the many works that have both informed and entertained me. I have consulted numerous printed works, some learned papers published in limited numbers, some only privately circulated, and some manuscript material. To acknowledge all sources when my head and my library shelves are occupied with every written word to which I have had access, is a nearly impossible task. I must however mention a particular indebtedness to Derk Kinnane Roelofsma's paper "Gaelic Elements in Irish Heraldry"; Dr McCarthy's paper on the Funeral Volume Entries: Genealogical Office Mss. 64 - 79.; Charles Lart's book *James Terry: Athlone Herald*; Edward MacLysaght's book *Irish Families*; and my gratitude to Hereward King for his lively illustrations. I must thank the staff of the National Library and the Genealogical Office, in particular Fergus Gillespie, Genealogical Officer at the Office of the Chief Herald, for his continual indulgence. Above all, my thanks to Donal F. Begley, Chief Herald of Ireland, for providing access to archive material, including the basis for the front cover design, and whose kindly guidance over a number of years has been invaluable.

An Introduction to Irish Heraldry

In Ireland we are fond of heraldry. Its graphic appeal is unquestionable, but more than that, we enjoy it for its association with history. To an Irishman any historic event is something that happened only the day before yesterday. Is this country unique in that conversations overheard in pubs or on the street are as likely to be about national, social or family history as about football or the news of the day? Those who can mark their own family's place in the wider scene of the history of the nation, or even that of the race, are fiercely proud of their roots and of their knowledge.

Even a short walk around Dublin, or indeed almost any Irish town, will provide examples of familial, corporate, ecclesiastical and territorial coats of arms. They will be found carved in stone, cast in bronze and iron, worked in stained glass or hand-painted wherever fancy may have dictated. For all that, few people understand all of heraldry's functions or full significance, or realize that it is a living, practical discipline that continues to fulfil its ages old purposes. The ability to read a coat of arms may provide access to information about the person who endowed the building on which it is carved, who signed the document to which it is affixed, is commemorated in the arms of an institution which bears his name. In our own day, to display arms on proper occasions is to create historical records for future enquirers.

Arms represent people. They need not be present, nor even living, but their arms at once represent identity and are a part of it. The national concern with Irish identity, both collective and personal, is well served by the science of heraldry.

Although our especial interest is in Irish heraldry it is impossible to examine it in isolation, that is, without being aware that heraldry is pan-European; a product of the cultural unity of continental Europe in medieval times, and in Ireland a bye-product of the attempt to draw us, however unwillingly, into the mainstream of that culture. Some familiarity with the background of heraldry as a whole is necessary, as is a definition of the term itself.

Heraldry or Armory?

Most people have encountered the word *heraldry* and probably *armory* as well. It may seem that the two are interchangeable, and for the present purpose they are. However it as well to understand that, to those who take more than the most casual interest in the subject, armory means the business of shields and the things which often, but not always, surround them, while the term heraldry encompasses a wide range of related matters.

It is generally understood that heraldry, in the way most commonly used, means the system of identification by the use of hereditary emblems. The practice of placing designs on shields and banners should more properly be called *armory* for the duties of a herald involve much more than the recording of coats of arms, and include carrying messages, being able to pronounce on matters of protocol and, in earlier times, counting and identifying the slain on the battlefield. Amongst our most important and extensive heraldic records are those kept by Irish heralds and their deputies whose duty it was to attend peacetime funerals of armigers. All that said, the word *heraldry* is so widely understood in its narrower sense that it may be confidently used.

We rightly associate heraldry with the crusading knights of the Middle Ages and the rite of chivalry whereby the newly invested knight exchanged his plain shield for one bearing a personal emblem. But despite continuous use for some eight hundred years we do not know exactly where and when heraldry originated. Claims made by ancient writers on the subject, that Old Testament references to banners are evidence of a far earlier origin than we know it to have, can be safely discounted. As late as the Norman invasion of England in 1066, heritable personal emblems were still unknown, though the painting of shields as an aid to recognition in battle was almost certainly practised; and the continental Celts had decorated their helmets and other war gear with representations of animals centuries earlier. These examples, however, do not fall within our definition of heraldry for such a design on a shield is unlikely to have remained in use for longer than the working life of that particular shield, perhaps less than one campaign, and like the early helmet crests of our Celtic ancestors lacked the essential factor of heritability. It will be seen, though, that certain ancient symbolism endured into heraldic times and, because of the continuing tradition of heraldry, survives to the present.

No reference to aid us in establishing a date for the earliest use of heraldry is to be found in the detailed contemporary accounts of the first two crusades. The historian Anna Comnena, daughter of the Byzantine emperor Alexius I, described the shields of the Frankish barbarians, as she termed the crusaders, quite specifically as "smooth and gleaming." Robert of Aix, who also left us first-hand descriptions of the shields of the first crusade mentions that they were painted various colours and sometimes sumptuously decorated with gold and gems, but makes no reference to heraldic bearings. The shields of the leaders of the second crusade, according to the engravings we have of the windows of the Abbey of St Denis near Paris (the actual windows having long since been destroyed) also indicate that heraldry was still unknown at that time.

However, by the time of the third crusade which began in 1189, it was already in use all over Europe. Why heraldry should have flowered so abundantly in so short a period has been the matter of much learned conjecture and discussion—and we are still no nearer any explanation other than the rather unsatisfactory one that Europe was waiting for some system of identification and that armory, when it appeared about the middle of the twelfth century, fitted the requirements of the time. By then the Normans had long accomplished the "just usurpation" of the throne of England and their descendants, with even flimsier legal justification, had arrived in Ireland, their shields and banners splendid with the colours and metals that remain in use today.

Though the Normans brought heraldry to Ireland it was not reserved to their use. If the rest of Europe had been ready for the recently evolved science of heraldry, so were the Gael who had been absorbing other European cultural influences through Britain, though slowly, for some centuries. This was not a one-way traffic. In fact there was a far stronger flow in the opposite direction. Throughout Europe Irish influence in the areas of devotion and scholarship was so powerful as to lead to the attempted suppression by Rome of the independent Irish Church after the Synod of Whitby in 664. Now five hundred years later a combination of circumstances (internal wars amongst the Irish, squabbles amongst the Welsh Normans, a certain insecurity on the part of the Anglo-Norman king of England and the continuing policy of the Church of Rome to be the only spiritual authority in Europe) all led to the Norman invasion and to foreign influence increasing at an entirely new pace. An examination of the use of heraldry by the Irish, its adoption and increasing importance, might almost allow a graph to be drawn charting the cultural and political changes that followed 1169. The existing culture that combined Druidism and Christianity; the subsequent racial mixing; the injection of English settlers and their laws and customs at several crucial stages in the country's history; the diaspora; the eventual departure of the invading power—all have worked their influences on Irish heraldry. Sometimes there are three discernible strains: Norman, Gaelic and Anglo-Irish. Sometimes they overlap to produce an armory as deserving of examination as Irish character itself.

The Shield and Its Charges

The kite-shaped Norman shield, widely familiar from the representation of the Battle of Hastings on the Bayeux Tapestry, was already going out of fashion by the time of the Norman invasion of Ireland. Sometimes it reached from shoulder to ankle and was curved to protect the user more fully. Improvements in body armour rendered such a large shield obsolete. These, like later shields, were basically of wood, though we know that by the beginning of the thirteenth century, and possibly before, pressed leather was in use for the figures upon the surface. A wooden shield, with or without leather decorations, requires metal reinforcement, either in the form of straps of steel or rows of rivets. We know that even in pre-heraldic times these were sometimes gilded or coloured differently from the base material. The geometric designs produced were not only decorative but identified the bearer to his followers and his opponents. So common were these simple markings that they became known in heraldic terminology as *ordinaries*. Their origin being so ancient, and the bearing of them unaccompanied by other charges an indication of the antiquity of the arms, they are sometimes called *The Honourable Ordinaries*.

The evolution of the visored helmet which completely concealed the knight's face increased the need for a means of ready recognition. The replacement of chain mail by plate armour in the mid-twelfth century allowed

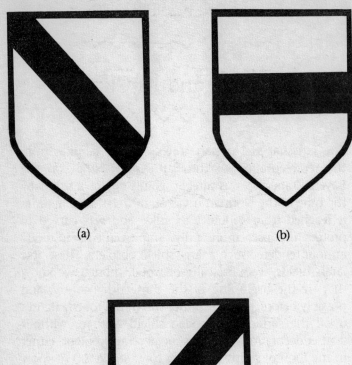

Some of the Honourable Ordinaries: (a) the Bend, (b) the Fess and (c) the Bend Sinister.

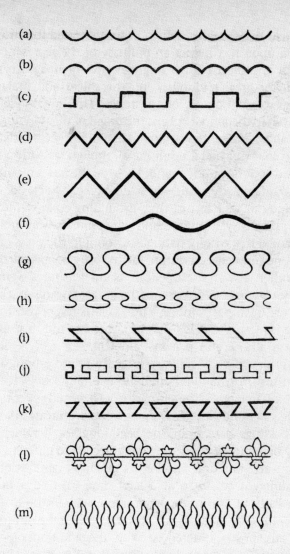

The Ordinaries may have their edges drawn in a variety of ways: (a) Engrailed, (b) Invected, (c) Embattled, (d) Indented, (e) Dancetty, (f) Wavy, (g) Nebuly (deep), (h) Nebuly (shallow), (i) Raguly, (j) Potenté, (k) Dovetailed, (l) Flory counter-flory, (m) Rayonné.

the shield to be smaller, which in turn dictated that the insignia upon it, whether an ordinary or the representation of an object (which might be real or imaginary) should, for greater visibility, fill the shield and make possible recognition at long distance. The function of early military heraldry explains the origin of the tradition in heraldic design that colour should not be placed upon colour nor metal upon metal, though, as with all rules, exceptions can be found. Likewise the base colour, the *field*, of an early shield was seldom green which does not stand out well against the surrounding countryside. It is equally easy to understand why animals were not represented in a wholly naturalistic form: in the press of battle one four-legged creature might easily be mistaken for another; a swan for a pelican. Natural features were therefore exaggerated, perhaps making a swan's neck abnormally long or painting a lion's claws bright red. In time a knight's shield, banner, surcoat and horse-trappings all bore his personal emblem.

Examples of early military heraldry found amongst the arms of Irish families are quite naturally associated with Norman names. The simplicity of Fitzgerald's *Argent, a saltire gules* and Burke's *Or, a cross gules* indicate that these bearings date from the beginnings of heraldry. Clearly branches of the same family needed to differentiate between one and another as much as families of quite different stock, so at a later time we find a de Burgh, Earl of Clanricarde, with a lion sable in the first quarter, for difference. Again, the arms of Burgh, Earl of Mayo are further differenced with the addition of a dexter hand apaumée sable in the second quarter. The arms of the Fitzgeralds of Desmond differ from those of their Leinster cousins by having a field of ermine.

A finite number of combinations of ordinary and colour would dictate the use of emblems, heraldically

The arms of Fitzgerald, Duke of Leinster. The simplicity of this coat (argent, a saltire gules) indicates its early origin, though this representation has certain marks of later heraldic art: a fanciful mantling falling from a helmet which, though a grilled helm, is of a design originating with the present illustrator. The cap within a coronet of rank is, strictly speaking, not supposed to be represented heraldically but, like the helm, often tempts the heraldic artist to excess.

called *charges*, other than ordinaries. From then onwards the possibilities were only limited by the imagination and taste of the bearer. The most important symbol of all in medieval Europe, the cross, though properly speaking an ordinary, appears in so many different forms as to almost defy catalaloging. Its use as an emblem for the cruasaders of pre-heraldic days is well known and it was naturally widely adopted, with one or another variation, as an heraldic bearing. Other obvious choices were weapons of war and castles; hounds, hawks and their various quarry species; some, like the cups of Butler, to indicate the bearer's office; some to make a pun on the bearer's name. Lions appear in the armory of all nations and in Ireland there seems to have been a fondness for them, usually rampant, and equally popular amongst those of all cultural backgrounds at every period. We meet, on the one hand, creatures of fantasy like the griffon and the mermaid, and on the other quite mundane objects such as stirrups, keys, millrinds and water bougets. Perhaps some of these were chosen arbitrarily or perhaps, at the time of their first use, they had some especial significance for the bearer that is now lost to us.

Oddly, certain charges that are common throughout Europe, including England, only rarely find their way into Irish armory. Considering the long period during which English customs influenced Irish life, some might expect Irish heraldry to be an imitation, even a miniature, of that of our neighbour which, by any reckoning, has been politically and culturally expansionist through most of its history. Instead, although we may cite some shields from every period that might be mistaken for English, we do not find our armory thick with clarions, caltraps, Catherine wheels and escarbuncles, nor indeed a host of other objects familiar only to the student of

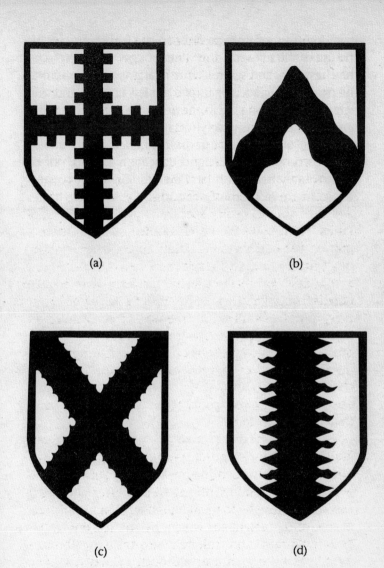

Some variations of the ordinaries: (a) Cross embattled, (b) chevron wavy; (c) saltire engrailed, (d) pale radiant (a variant of rayonné).

heraldry. It is certainly possible to cite Irish examples of the use of the maunch, the water bouget, the fetterlock, the chess rook and several other charges common across the channel, but such examples are few enough and the heraldist searching Irish armory for such heraldic obscurities as fleams and fylfots may give himself a long task. Most of the objects upon Irish shields are familiar but their complete significance is seldom known, nor is it commonly realised that heraldic shields were not carried in battle by the Gaelic Irish.

Arms, Territory and the Family

The fact that early heraldic documents sometimes describe and illustrate arms originating in countries other than those in which these Rolls of Arms were compiled is of particular interest in relation to Irish heraldry. In the *Armorial Wijnbergen*, a document in the French language dating from about 1275 and now preserved in Holland, we find the earliest reference to the arms of *Le Roi d'Irlande* which are given as *Azure, a harp or*. In non-heraldic language that is simply a gold harp on a blue background. These are still, basically, the arms of Ireland and, for the period of office, the arms of each president. These few facts tell us at once of heraldry's antiquity, its pan-European presence, its ancient territorial aspect and its continuing use.

In Gaelic Ireland land was the property of an extended family group or *sept*. Though lesser chiefs might acknowledge their more powerful neighbours as overlords, each septal territory was autonomous. The High Kingship of Ireland was an institution of quite late foundation, largely titular, and should not be understood as ever having been a universally recognised authority. However, in the feudal structure of other medieval European states land was held in return for military service when the king should require it. The greater in size the feudal fief, the greater would be the number of men its lord was obliged to supply. A baron would be bound to muster a particular number of knights and each knight would in turn have to be able to call upon a specific number of foot soldiers. Clearly the foot soldier had no need of armorial bearings. His only concern was to be able to recognise those on his master's banner and follow wherever it led him.

Thus arms came to be identified with territory and passed with the territory from one person to another. When such a transfer occurred other than through inheritance by direct succession, one man might find himself with two coats of arms while another could lose the right to the use of arms by which his family had been identified for generations. This confused situation which negated the entire point of heraldry, identification, was debated by the Parliament of Paris in 1383. It was decided that arms should follow the blood rather than the fief: that is, that arms should belong to a family and not the land it occupied. As France was both cultural and geographical centre of medieval Europe this view was disseminated throughout Christendom.

In Ireland we share the widespread custom of regarding all male descendents of the original bearer of arms as being armigerous and having a right to some share of use of the basic family arms, also called the *pronominal* coat. (The matter of the arms of a lady merits separate treatment.) If we recall the Gaelic custom of holding land to be common property and the fact that rulers were elected from within a dynastic group, the matter of the heritability of the original coat becomes as confused as the situation which required examination elsewhere in Europe. A Gaelic chief who adopted arms by virtue of his position may well have been succeeded by someone other than his son: perhaps his brother, a cousin, even his father. Who then would have inherited his arms: his son or his successor in office? We may only surmise about the opinions that may have been formed in such circumstances at that time. The only certainty is that members of the same family did bear coats of arms that are sometimes quite obviously variations on a graphic and probably symbolic theme. While it is true that in heraldic law, and common sense, a coat of arms can only belong to one person at time, the head of the family, it is equally true that in Ireland all members of the family feel a measure of proprietorial interest in their chief's arms which serve as a focus for the family rather than just the mark of an individual. This familial aspect tends to assume a greater importance than the essentially temporary guardianship of a piece of family property by the clan's chief.

That said, if we are to avoid confusion between one member of a family and another, there must be some readily discernible difference between your arms and those of your elder brother, your younger brother and your cousins to several degrees. For this reason the system of *differencing* evolved and specialists, heralds, exist to advise on how best to retain the essential function of armory: recognition of an individual. That you may care to be recognised as a member of a particular family is understandable (one might say that in Ireland the lack of such a desire would be regarded as suspicious) but you may not use another person's arms.

The Status of Armiger

How then does a family acquire a coat of arms, and what formalities are involved? The power to grant arms belongs to the state; historically in the person of its sovereign. In a democracy, such as this republic, sovereign power resides with its people who delegate authority to the elected government. Heraldic authority is in turn delegated by the government to an officer of arms and the right to bear arms depends on a grant from such an officer. Thereafter arms may be borne by direct male descent from the original grantee.

In early days arms were not granted by any authority but simply assumed as the user required them, primarily to draw attention to himself in battle. In peacetime the display of arms on every possible occasion was a continual assertion of his status as a member of the knightly class: a person of consequence who could be called upon to defend country and dependents. It is hardly surprising to find that ruling powers decided quite early that records should be kept of such influential subjects, their feudal responsibilities and related privileges, and which of the family would, in time, inherit those duties. The cataloguing of hereditary coats of arms was an essential part of this and naturally led to the bearing of arms being subject to legal regulation.

By a grant of arms one might, in those days, be said to have been invested with a form of nobility, though from Tudor times the application of the term was confined to the peerage. Nowadays a grant of arms honours its recipient but cannot be said to ennoble. Considering the implications that the word "nobility," with its understood relationship to inherited privilege, had for most Irish people during much of our history, it is natural enough that today's egalitarianism makes us somewhat shy of its use. However, it is worthwhile, in passing, to observe that its Latin source (*nobilis*-=known) gives some insight into the origin of the term and the concept it denotes when used in its oldest and broadest sense. One was *known* to one's ruler; *known* to be liable for military service or parliamentary duties. In medieval times it was by no means a status universally aspired to, any more than some of today's citizens welcome the attention of the Revenue Commissioners. That said, there were and are many families that through successive generations did not seek to avoid military and civic duties and took considerable pride in the fact that their arms, displayed on an occasion of state, had been borne on ancient battlefields. To bear arms was and remains an expression of a wish to be identified with one's country's affairs and history, for no one can have arms forced upon him.

For those who cannot prove descent from an earlier armiger and feel that they have reached a state in life that merits the distinction of a coat of arms, the first step toward a new grant is a petition expressing one's desire to bear arms. The petitioner and an heraldic officer develop a design which does not infringe any other armiger's rights and it is conveyed by a legal instrument, much like the deeds of a house, to the petitioner. After its registration all rights and usage are vested in the grantee, his heirs and successors. Like any other legal process this involves a specialist's examination of earlier documents; it requires the creation of the document itself, in this case a fine specimen of calligraphy and emblazonment, and appropriate fees are involved.

The aspiring armiger is not only subscribing to an historical tradition of affirming solidarity with the state and its ideals, but a tradition that is not without its egalitarian aspect: arms granted yesterday have no less a value in law than those borne by a descendant of a knight who stepped ashore with Strongbow, anymore than the bicycle I bought last week is less mine than the one you have owned for ten years. Yours, I allow, may well have a more interesting history but its legal status as property is not enhanced by the fact that you inherited it from your father and he from his who, in turn, received it by the grace of the King of England.

In the Republic there is no machinery for conferring other hereditary honours. The style, *Chief of the Name*, can of course only be confirmed, not conferred. One may quite properly use titles conferred by foreign powers and enjoy whatever privileges attach to them in their country of origin, but in Ireland the armiger has no hope of further elevation and his descendants will find themelves with no privileges but the right to display their arms on appropriate occasions, and the perhaps greater one of an increased sense of history.

The Office of Herald

It is too simple to say, as have previous heraldists, that Irish heraldry follows broadly English lines. It would be more exact to say that because of our shared experience with the English, the imposition of Norman rule and culture, that the heraldry of the two countries has a common origin. Our long subsequent rule by England quite naturally imposed its imprint upon all our administrative machinery. However when speaking of heraldry it is well to note that if there are administrative similarities there are also enough differences to make it necessary to qualify certain general statements about the herald's work when speaking of the Irish situation. Like much else that came to us with, and as a result of, the invasion, heraldry has been adapted to Irish ways and uses. A turbulent history contributed much to the way imported legislation of all kinds was applied: how effectively enforced, how modified to fit existing circumstances. Though the post of herald is of foreign origination several of the means of discharging his duties have long been peculiarly Irish.

The Chief Herald of Ireland is the holder of the oldest state office. Although the post has been called by various names during the five centuries through which its twenty-three incumbents have supervised the use of arms in this country, the duties have remained the same, mainly the granting of arms, the confirmation of earlier grants and the recording of genealogies.

Although no Irish herald ever officiated at a tournament it was certainly the tourney that raised heralds from a status no more exalted than that of itinerant entertainers to that of the important officials which they became. It is likely that some did begin their careers as actors and acrobats. Their travels from one great house to another would have provided the opportunity to familiarise themselves with the arms and genealogy of many important families, and would surely have presented chances to serve their patrons by conveying news to the next castle which they were to visit. Tournaments provided great opportunities for heraldic display, and indeed contributed to the necessity for a means of recognition. A knight completely encased in heavy jousting armour could be identified only by his bearings, and the ability to recognise them and proclaim his name was a very saleable skill.

If, as is believed, the word herald is derived from the German *haren*, to cry out, then it is eminently applicable to those who, to our certain knowledge, were engaged to announce the date and place of approaching tournaments which they would themselves attend, there to add all possible pomp to the occasion by introducing the contestants, lauding their past achievements and doubtless those of their ancestors. Intimacy with the armorial bearings of all present would obviously have been of the greatest importance. In the early days of heraldry they were freelance operators in the casual employment of wealthy knights who rewarded them handsomely, for largesse was one of the chivalric virtues. In time great magnates kept heralds as full-time members of their households and entrusted them with such duties as carrying confidential messages from province to province and even between countries. A herald's importance quite naturally increased in proportion to the importance of his master. When heralds became regular members of royal establishments they had reached the top of their profession and were regarded as functionaries of considerable importance. They became, in fact, a diplomatic corps with appropriate privileges. To harm a herald was regarded as a most serious crime. Just as now, when the members of a nation's foreign service are classed as non-combatants excluded from whatever disputes their country may have with another, the herald was immune from all danger. Territorial boundaries and any disagreements between their princely masters were not necessarily of personal importance to them and heralds representing warring powers were known to meet and socialise, for their trustworthiness was beyond question.

The ability to recognise instantly the banners and shields of an army in the field, to identify the fallen and later to give an account of the battle to chroniclers; the duty of supervising the exchange of prisoners; the increasing social importance of heraldry in peacetime, all added to the demand for the heralds' professional skills and it was inevitable that they should become the arbiters of all matters relating to the use of arms and the protocol of the hierarchical social structure of feudal times. Probably because of the profession's origin, there appears to have been little bar to anyone becoming a herald, short of his being a convicted criminal. Apart from taking holy orders it was perhaps the peasant's only way of rising out of the social class into which he was born. In a matter of two centuries the herald's profession achieved the unlikely evolution from travelling player to important state official.

A dispute concerning the use of the same coat of arms by three different people is recorded as having been adjudicated upon in England in 1390. From this we gather that by then arms were regarded in law as property and that the Crown could and did grant arms and exercised ultimate control in heraldic matters. From the lack of any mention of heraldic officers in the detailed records of these proceedings, which lasted five years and cost several fortunes, we may assume that no such posts had been created there at that date. It may reasonably be supposed that the heralds of the time were consulted, though they would still have been members of the royal household rather than state functionaries. In 1484 Richard III established a College of Arms, so elevating his personal servants to an official status. The most important of these were called Kings of Heralds of Arms, later abbreviated to "King of Arms". It was commonplace at that time for all chiefs of their trades or professions to be called "King" and we know of, amongst others, Kings of Fools and Kings of Beggars.

The first reference to such an officer of arms seemingly for Ireland is from 1382 when one John Chandos was appointed "Ireland King of Arms." It is fairly certain that he never came to Ireland and unfortunately little is known of the man or his office, though he was followed by a succession of people bearing the title, who seem to have been regarded as members of the English college, until the time of Edward IV when a Thomas Ashwell was appointed. Thereafter it is not known whether the office continued to exist. In 1552 the post of Ulster King of Arms was created by Edward VI and in his journal we find:

Feb. 2nd. There was a King of Arms made for Ireland, whose name was Ulster, and his province was all Ireland; and he was fourth King of Arms, and first Herald of Ireland.

Why this herald was named after the ancient kingdom of Ulster, rather than "Ireland King" like his predecessors, is not known. In time the Irish heraldic establishment built up to a body of five permanent officers. Apart from Ulster King of Arms there was Athlone Pursuivant; the two heralds of the order of St Patrick, called Dublin Herald and Cork Herald; and a Cork Pursuivant of the order. During the period of British rule Ulster was the Lord Lieutenant's most senior member of staff, the only permanent one and next in order of precedence to the Viceroy himself. His duties were not just to "inspect, determine and correct arms, to impose differences on arms, and to grant Letters Patent of arms", being also concerned with the ordering of state ceremonies and the issuing of proclamations. His opportunities to inspect and correct were limited by the political disturbances that occurred in every generation and the generally poor communications throughout the country. To maintain control of the use of arms the system of a herald or his local deputy attending the funerals of armigers was devised. In this way records of arms in use were kept up-to-date and appropriate taxes enabled to be collected, though often with difficulty. The lack of complete records resulted in Ulster being allowed extensive powers of confirmation of arms (far beyond those of any English herald) to those who asserted their hereditary use of arms without previous registration.

Throughout Ireland's troubled history, the fluctuations of English power and influence, the period of Parliamentary rule, the Restoration of the monarchy and the subsequent change of dynasty from Stuart to Hanoverian, the tenure of this office continued without interruption. It is interesting to note in passing that Cromwell's appointee, Richard Carney, who was removed at the demise of the Commonwealth, was later returned to

Office of the Chief Herald of Ireland

Ulster King of Arms

office under Charles II on the resignation of his replacement, Richard St.George, in 1683. St George too is worth remark, for his family included no fewer than five Kings of Arms including his son, another Richard, who was appointed Ulster in 1692.

This post continued in its original form until the death of its last incumbent, Sir Neville Wilkinson, in 1940, long after the foundation of the Free State. Sir Neville had been appointed for life and as this was a Crown appointment the government of the new state, still at that time a British dominion, had no power to remove him, nor any urgent need to do so. The office still exists but has been absorbed into that of Norroy King of Arms while the subsidiary posts of the old Ulster establishment were allowed to lapse. Norroy and Ulster's province is the north of England and the six counties of Northern Ireland. In 1943 heraldic duties in relation to *Saorstat Éireann* were taken over by the newly created Chief Herald of Ireland and the Office of Arms at Dublin Castle became the Genealogical Office. Copies of the entire collection of heraldic documents which successive Ulster Kings of Arms had amassed over four centuries were lodged with Norroy and Ulster's office at the College of Arms in London.

Of recent years the records of The Office of Arms have been removed to the Genealogical Office's new location at Kildare Street. Though the present Dublin Office is a somewhat more modest establishment than previously, with no regalia, colourful titles or elaborate protocol, it is no less active. Its staff of ten, the principals of which are the Chief Herald and a Genealogical Officer, provide a focus for the worldwide interest in Irish heraldry and genealogy.

So, in a small country, comprised of two main administrative areas, we have two independent heraldic authorities. While it can be said that the Chief Herald has for his jurisdiction the national territory as defined by the Constitution, the entire island of Ireland, and that this heraldic authority can properly extend to those of Irish extraction throughout the world, particularly in those countries where no recognised heraldic authority exists, in practice he and Norroy and Ulster recognise the validity of each other's grants. The existing territorial border certainly marks the limit of Norroy and Ulster's authority but it is not unusual for Northern armigers to address their enquiries to Dublin as the Office by which their arms were originally granted. Paradoxically, the grant to Stormont was made at Dublin Castle, though this was of course between the dates of the division of the country and the division of heraldic responsibility. More recent cross-border grants are not unusual, in particular those to Roman Catholic bishops, though religious or political views do not stop others from seeing the elder of the two offices as being the one which should govern heraldic affairs for all Irish people.

It may be thought more normal for those resident in the North, or overseas residents of Northern extraction, to address their petitions to Norroy and Ulster's Office, while those of families originating in the twenty-six counties should deal with Dublin. Apart from such a procedure being far too simple a solution for Irish taste, the present situation has the merit of retaining something of heraldry's trans-national character and the heralds' custom of operating on a different plane from that of their masters.

Arms and the Law

An heraldic achievement is property, cultural and intellectual property, and is regarded so in law. This property is created by the desire of the grantee and the consent of the state. The fact that the right to private property is guaranteed by the constitution clearly has implications for the armiger and those officials who administer heraldry in Ireland: the government and its officers of arms. The position may be simplified by saying that registration of arms is the recording of their ownership. The use of registered arms by a person unable to prove proprietary right is legally actionable misappropriation. A coat of arms unknown to the official heraldic authority, unregistered arms, has no legal existence.

Something has been said of the procedures associated with a grant to an individual. In the case of a corporate entity, whether a civic body or a commercial company, resolutions in council are required to initiate a petition for a formal grant. To whom the use and enjoyment of the arms is granted is clearly laid out. It may apply to a town or borough's corporation or council; perhaps to its citizens as well.

Although the Chief Herald retains and exercises the right to regulate the use of arms there is widespread assumption of arms in Ireland. The belief commonly held both here and in England, that each name has a coat of arms which may be borne by any person of that name, is quite contrary to heraldic law. One recent writer on the subject, the late L. G. Pine, astutely described this as, "a theory devised by the simple-minded and utilised by the business-minded." In Ireland this misconception is in part compounded by some widely read words of the late Dr Edward MacLysaght who was appointed Chief Herald in 1943. Though a most accomplished genealogist, MacLysaght was considered by some heraldic authorities to have been mistaken in his opinion that certain ancient Irish coats might be regarded as appertaining to any member of a sept. This was of course merely an opinion and there was certainly no act of the Office of the Chief Herald which binds his successors to any policy based upon that opinion. Indeed, he was careful to point out that it did not imply a blanket licence to appropriate or assume arms, though it has been widely, and sometimes culpably, construed as such. He also roundly condemned any suggestion that "clan arms", analagous to the clan badges of the Scots, had any existence at all, if only because the use of the term *clan* tends to suggest that a clan system similar to that of Scotland existed here at some time.

Whatever may be said in mitigation of persons who, quite simply, know no better, it seems unlikely that those who sell to absolutely anybody what purports to be the customer's family coat have never delved a little into the matter from which they derive their living. They must be aware that the chances of their supplying the correct coat of arms to a person of whom they know little except the surname, are thousands to one against. In the United States there are those who have it that an offer to "mail you your family arms for $X if you send us your name" is a fraudulent use of the mails. There is certainly a case for any arms acquired over a counter being accompanied by the motto, *Caveat emptor*.

As there are few provable Gaelic chiefs surviving, the use of anciently recorded coats by persons who co-incidentally bear the same name as the original armiger continues because, in most cases, there is no one to complain. What they are in effect doing by assuming these derelict arms is assuming the chieftainship of that name, without acceptable proof to substantiate the claim. Although there exists in Gaelic armory a tradition of expressing one's wish to be known as related to a particular, perhaps famous, family, to do so by the use of an undifferenced coat of arms without provable descent most certainly has no legal sanction. Quite apart from any legal considerations, to misappropriate another's arms shows, in the would-be armiger, a scant respect for his true ancestors and though he may not be prosecuted he may well be ridiculed.

Though an Irish or English armiger might choose to allow others to claim his property as their own, no such liberties would be tolerated in Scotland. The arbiter of all heraldic matters there, Lyon King of Arms, has a right in law to order the removal of unregistered arms. Should a resident of his jurisdiction display a spurious or a bogus coat, Lyon King may send a deputy with a blowtorch, a hammer and chisel, or whatever else is needed to remove it. And his powers do not end there: the Lord Lyon is a judge and has the right to fine and imprison those who disobey him. Heralds in other countries might be forgiven should they view his authority with some envy.

Heraldic lawlessness has its limits in Ireland also. If, for example, I should be so enthused by the heraldic achievement of my bank as to have it printed upon my writing paper, that armigerous body, with the support of the Chief Herald, would soon order me to cease and desist, for to use another's arms implies action on the armiger's behalf.

While misappropriation of arms is always wrong, the assumption of arms in Ireland might *almost* be said to have respectable precedents. In fact it began to be practised here when it had already been forbidden in other European countries. Because the Normans never established complete control of Ireland (and indeed, their political successors, the British, did not arrive at that position until the seventeenth century*) Gaelic chieftains continued to be regarded as kings, if minor ones, not only by their own people but by the invaders. Who then, in those days, had a better right to assume arms? If there is no evidence of such Gaelic rulers allowing their followers to use these arms or a portion of them, there is nothing in heraldic tradition that would have precluded their doing so. We have evidence enough that great feudal lords in England did exactly that, which accounts for certain charges being common to several families which originated in the same area. The imitation of the arms of England by the O'Brien kings of Connacht after their surrender and regrant is an example of the loyalty of the armiger being acknowledged in his arms. To abandon arms anciently and legitimately assumed in favour of others denoting allegiance is truly indicative of a resignation to the new order.

It was the opinion of Oswald Barron (who was earlier this century widely considered to be the greatest living authority on medieval heraldry) that,

> A coat is not held from the Crown, but is simply a piece of personal property, the right to which depends simply upon the user and the right as against others upon prior assumption.

O'Brien (ancient)

O'Brien (modern)

This was certainly true in the earliest days of heraldry and to a much later date in Ireland. It remains true in those countries which lack any official regulation of arms. However, in this country one must have proper regard for long established custom, practice and, of course, the law of the land.

*It is worth remark that despite the fact that the Normans arrived in Ireland with state-of-the-art military technology and the experience of the first two crusades, the subjection of this tiny island, lacking a central administration or any cohesive political force, took more than four centuries.

Gaelic Heraldry

Irish military techniques and equipment were far less sophisticated than those of the Normans. The failure to adopt the stirrup left the mounted warrior unable to couch a lance. Upon this use of the weapon rests the evolution of the Norman body armour, helmet and shield shape. The Irish carried their spears overarm, avoided pitched battles and made much use of landscape features to attack moving columns. The war-games of the tournament field which continued elsewhere in Europe down to Tudor times were not part of the training or amusement of the Irish cavalryman, whose weapons and tactics remained virtually unchanged until late in the sixteenth century. The rich display of heraldic decoration at the tourney, which did so much to popularise the use of heraldry and increase the importance of the herald's work in other countries, contributed nothing to the adoption of heraldry by the native Irish or the development of the distinctive Gaelic school.

This did not prevent the use of heraldry for other than military applications. The main purpose to which the native Irish put the science was in the design of signets. In an age of almost universal illiteracy, armorial bearings were used to attest documents and identify property. There grew up a characteristic and independent Gaelic armory which owed little to the traditions of Norman heraldry and for its symbolology drew heavily

The arms of Hugh Reamher O'Neill, after a fourteenth century seal impression.

The arms of Rotherick (Ruari) O'Kennedy, from a seal of 1356.

upon pre-Norman, pre-Christian, perhaps pre-Celtic history, legend and religion.

The earliest recorded arms of an Irish prince are those of Hugh O'Neill, King of Ulster, who died in 1325. Impressions of his seal show the heraldic use of the most famous and possibly the most ancient of Gaelic symbols, the open right hand. The oldest document relevant to Irish heraldry in the possession of the National Library is a treaty of 1356 bearing the seal of Roderick O'Kennedy. In it he is acknowledged by the Earl of Ormond as "chief of his nation." On this shield are two combatant lions, with what is possibly a sword in between them. By the sixteenth century several important dynasties were using the same arms in successive generations. For example, the arms on a fifteenth century seal, that of Donald Reagh MacMurrough Kavanagh, which shows a lion passant on a shield supported by two lions, appear again on that of his grandson, Murrough MacMurrough Kavanagh, attached to a treaty of 1515. Such arms, though borne by assumption rather than as a result of a grant by the Crown, were recognised and recorded by the English-appointed heralds in Dublin, just as would have been those arms originating abroad which came to their notice.

Although much of the Gaelic culture still survived it appears that social changes were occurring and that the adoption and adaption of heraldry was linked to an emerging feudalism fashioned after that which the Irish chiefs saw working beneficially for Norman leaders. Hugh O'Neill, already mentioned, introduced succession by lineal descent into that family, rather than the *deirbfhine* system under which the chief was elected from amongst a dynastic group, and similar changes were happening elsewhere in the country.

It must be said that not all ruling families adopted

the use of arms or other alien institutions, and those who did created a school of heraldry with its roots deep in historical memory. In spite of the conversion of the Irish to Christianity they were still steeped in pagan tradition and their strong affection for that heritage found a new means of expression in armory.

Some Gaelic Charges

The armory of the Normans originated as a part of military science and its practical application was the greatest factor in its evolution. That of the Gael had practical but different applications so did not share the restraints imposed by military heraldry's considerations. Its charges were not chosen for their ability to be recognised under difficult conditions. Readily distinguishable they had to be and doubtless were, but most readily so to those who shared the culture of their bearers. This Gaelic armory was not simply a depiction of a fighting-man's identifying emblem. Its literary, historical and religious allusions impart a character at once intellectual and mystical.

All but a few details of druidic religion are likely to remain forever a mystery to us. What we do know is that primitive religion and mythology are inextricably bound together, that the gods of early times become the heroes of myth and legend, and that some of our Celtic mythology survived to be written down, ironically, by Christian monks of later times. Though these pious scribes were sometimes inclined to impose the mores of their own time on the warriors of our heroic age, the core of these sagas remain. These records are not the only means by which the tales of Cuchulain, The Red Branch, Fionn and the Fianna reach us: a lively oral tradition has also helped to preserve them, in various versions, into our own times. Certain classics of Celtic literature are as familiar to many Irish people today as they were to our ancestors. How much more realistic must they have been to a people who still inhabited the same wild world as their heroes and had not accumulated a further eight centuries of alien cultural influence? There can be little doubt that Gaelic heraldry is full of literary allusions. Though there are some that we may never decipher, others we can identify with some certainty. Let us examine some of the most common charges in Gaelic coats of arms. Amongst them are the dexter hand; the boar; the stag; the oak tree; the salmon and the serpent.

The hand is a sun symbol common to many cultures and there is ample evidence that the Celts worshipped Belinus, a sun god. Even St Patrick in his *Confession* provides testimony to the fact with:

> The splendour of the material sun which rises every day at the bidding of God will pass away and those that worship it will go into dire punishment; whereas the true sun, Christ, whom we Christians worship, shall endure forever.

He would hardly have troubled to issue his warning had sun worship not been commonplace in the Ireland of his day.

In later times the hand was said to represent *Dexter Dei* = The Right Hand of God. Though it is true that in early Christian symbolology the open right hand was used to represent God the Father, this is in all likelihood a Christianisation of an earlier tradition. The conjecture has been made by some scholars of Gaelic armory that the hand also denotes royal descent in that it can be read as a symbol of the *deirbfhine*. It has been suggested that the palm of the hand represents the common

The arms of O'Sullivan Mor in which several important Celtic symbols appear.

ancestor and that the three joints of the fingers represent sons, grandsons, and great-grandsons. Only those within this degree of kinship were *rig danae*, eligible for the sacred office of king.

The appearance of the dexter hand on the seal of Hugh O'Neill has been mentioned, but there is a tradition that the emblem was previously associated with the family Macgennis and passed to the O'Neills when they replaced the Macgennises as the dominant family of Ulster. Whether or not this is so, it has ever since been used by those claiming a right to rule that part of Ireland. Superimposed on the cross of the Burkes it forms the Arms of Ulster, of which more will be said elsewhere.

The red hand borne on an inescutcheon by baronets is our same symbol, though having travelled an anomalous route to arrive there. To help finance his plans for the settlement of Ireland, James I instituted the Order of Baronets by a patent of 1611. By payment of three years' wages for thirty soldiers at eightpence per day, a gentleman of property purchased an hereditary knighthood and the right to augment his shield with the red hand. This is almost always a sinister hand but some Irish baronets have used the dexter. This order was originally to have been limited to two hundred persons but market demand brought about its expansion. This crass sale of titles is much removed from both the traditions of chivalry and those of the Gaelic heroic sagas one would more properly associate with this charge.

The matter of the origin of the red hand should not be left without telling the stirring, though unlikely, tale of two Gaelic chieftains racing their boats in competition for the rich lands of Ulster. Whichever touched land first was to claim all. The O'Neill, seeing his opponent begin to take the lead, drew his sword and hacked off his hand which he hurled onto the shore ahead of his rival! Much as one may wish to believe the story it must be mentioned that the hand is not only the emblem of the descendents of Niall Noígiallach. It occurs in the arms of many other Gaelic families of which O'Reilly, Keogh, McCartan, McAuley, McDonnell, Geoghegan, Dunleavy and Daly are but a few of the possible examples. The mailed hand that is common as a crest amongst certain Gaelic families should not be dismissed as being of non-Gaelic origin because of the presence of Norman armour. The substitution of an armoured hand for the natural one is documented in the case of several Scottish coats and there is every reason to suppose that such a change could have taken place in Irish heraldry.

The boar was an object of reverence to the Celts. The strength and sheer savagery of this animal would have appealed to a race of warriors whose favourite peacetime activity was hunting but we can detect more here than the admiration of the hunter for his quarry. The boar's bristles, like the fingers of the hand, suggested the rays of the sun. Whether the boar was worshipped we do not know, but Celtic warriors of earlier times certainly wore figurines of it, presumably in the belief that its power, both physical and magical, would be imparted to the wearer. Their spears were decorated with boars and, although it was hardly done for the purpose of recognition, a shield similarly adorned found in the River Witham has survived from Celtic Britain. It has been mentioned that some European Celts also crested their helmets with representations of boars. All looked forward to an endless feast of pork after death.

The pursuit of a huge supernatural boar features in the myths of Ireland and Wales and the story of Diarmod and Grainne with its tragic hunt of the great boar of Ben Bulben, probably the god/hero Fionn magically transformed, is one of the classic tales of mythological tradition, versions of which are also known throughout Gaelic Scotland. It is no surprise to find the boar surfacing as an heraldic device for Irish families such as O'Sullivan, MacDonagh, MacDermot, Doran, Crowley, Cassidy and many more.

Likewise the stag, associated by the continental Celts with the horned god Cernunnos, frequently occurs as a mystical animal in the Fenian sagas. There recurs the theme of a stag which leads the hunters a wild chase before escaping into the woodland. Usually the deer is a magically changed lady who has some object such as a ring with the power to impart all knowledge to the wearer. Confronted by the heroes she is never willing to part with her secrets.

First a god, later the object of mystical story, in heraldic times the stag appears again as the emblem on the shields of certain Gaelic families. The deer (in Irish, *fiadh*) of the ancient arms of O'Doherty seems to make a punning allusion to that family's known descent from the sub-clan *Fiamhin*. It occurs also in the arms of those who claim descent from the very founders of the Irish race. The McCarthy and O'Connell families are amongst those that call themselves *sinsear clanna mileadh*—the elders of Milesius.

Others claim a yet longer pedigree. Some of the families that chose the hound and the oak tree as their charges appear to have used them to recall their descent from the *Erreainn* who inhabited parts of the south of Ireland before the Gael. The ancestor-god of the Erreainn, Curoi Mac Daire, has in his name the elements of a pun on the Gaelic words for hound, *cú*, and oak, *daire*. It is unlikely that the same thought did not occur to those who spoke the language every day. A certainty is that hounds were always important to them. Long lists of

Fionn's favourite hounds appear in the Fenian tales and from that time to our own the Irish greyhound, of one or another type, has been a prized possession. So highly regarded were the ancient breed of wolfhound that their export was forbidden and even as late as Tudor times they were an appropriate royal gift, for Henry VIII is recorded as having made such a present, and under a royal patent, to certain Spanish aristocrats.

With and without the greyhound, boar or stag, the oak, a powerful symbol of the druidic tree cult, figures prominently in Gaelic armory. We see it in the arms of Hegarty, Geraghty, Boyle, O'Callaghan, O'Connor and many more Irish families. Though the druids kept their secrets well in their own time and later researchers have been able to discover little of what was actually believed, a tree that under *brehon* law could merit the death sentence for those who felled it was obviously of great importance to them. Into historical times certain oak groves lent something of their sacred character to the rite of the investiture of rulers. That at Rathcrogan was associated from early times with the kingship of Connacht. More recently, well into the Christian period, the O'Connors were invested to that office near to its site.

The oak was not alone in having special virtues attributed to it and the relative nobility of certain trees, starting with the oak, was encoded in law. Not only were the initial letters of tree names used to compose much of the earliest Celtic alphabet but their names were used as a shorthand for the thirteen months of the Celtic calendar.

The salmon is seen in the arms of O'Neill, Donnelly, MacLoughlin and numerous other Gaelic families. It is unlikely to have been chosen without some thought for, like the oak groves, salmon pools were mystical places linked with the sacred office of king. It is well known that one Gaelic leader, on defeating another and taking his territory, would destroy his sacred salmon pools. Clearly the salmon had some great significance that is now lost to us. We may be sure that the fish was associated with great wisdom and the story of how Fionn acquired that wisdom by burning his thumb whilst cooking the Salmon of Knowledge is told and retold in several versions. As Dagda, the supreme Celtic deity, was also regarded as the repository and fount of all wisdom, it is difficult not to feel that there existed some connection between the two.

The presence in Irish story of a young maiden called Liban who was saved from a flood by the miraculous transformation of her body, with the exception of her face and breasts, to that of a salmon, reminds us that a mermaid is the crest of MacInerney, O'Byrne and O'Cullen. The two last septs inhabited part of south County Wicklow much associated with mermaids and called *Mureday*, land of the sea-goddess.

The frequent occurrence of the snake in Gaelic heraldry may be found puzzling to some, partly because Ireland has no snakes and partly because the Christian symbol for the devil would seem to have far too much importance to a people noted for their Christian piety. Every Irishman knows that Saint Patrick banished snakes from the country, and every zoologist knows that Ireland had no snakes to start with. Clearly, Patrick drove out snake worship which the continental ancestors of the Gael had brought with them and, in all likelihood, destroyed its cult objects. None the less, some seven or more centuries after Patrick, when heraldry appeared in Ireland, though their goddess-spirit Brigit had long been absorbed into Christian mythology, snakes, a symbol of renewal and revitalization, were still much in the Irish

The arms of O'Friel. The hand grasping a cross is a characteristically Gaelic charge, in this case indicating collateral descent
with Saint Columbkille.

consciousness. They, and their near relation the lizard, appear in the arms of at least two dozen Gaelic families which include O'Sullivan, O'Donovan, O'Dea, Mooney and Corrigan. It has been suggested that the lizard was chosen in preference to the snake by those who wished to show some deference to Christian beliefs but not lose sight of their pagan heritage.

The Christianisation of earlier traditions is seen in the attempt to explain away this fondness for a strong pagan symbol in a Christian art form, by the story repeated by historians as late as the last century. It was claimed that Gaodhel, the ancestor of the Gael said to have given his name to the entire people, was bitten by a snake in the Egyptian desert but was cured by a touch of the staff of the prophet Moses, and that the event is widely commemorated in Irish armory. We may be as sceptical about this tale as we are of the descent from Old Testament characters that ninth century Irish genealogists attributed to their royal masters.

The Gaelic word *leomhan* can mean both "lion" and "warrior" and is applied to several heroes of Irish mythology. However, those named Kelly, Murphy, Malone, Kavanagh, O'Flaherty, O'Dwyer or indeed any of the many Gaelic names that have been associated with this bearing should not assume descent from one of our legendary heroes, for the lion is a common charge in the armory of all countries. That is not to say that it did not have some special significance for the Gael. We have seen that they regarded the lion as the embodiment of courage, and which Irish chieftain would not have cared to have this quality linked to his name through his coat of arms? In the same context might be mentioned the griffin (in Irish, *gríobh*) which as well as being known as another sun-symbol, is in Irish a synonym for "hero". Small wonder at its appearance as charge or crest in the

MacDonnell (of Clare and Connaught). Christian and earlier symbols appear side by side in this distinctively Gaelic coat.

arms of Griffin, Ryan, O'Keefe, O'Meehan and several more Irish families.

Swords also occur in the heraldry of every nation but their presence in Irish armory prompts one to recall that one of our lion-warriors of the Fianna, Dermot O'Dyna, is said to have had his swords (named the Great Fury and the Little Fury) as a gift from the god of the sun. Cuchulainn's magical sword, which shone brightly at night, is not the only such weapon possessed by an Irish hero: MacCecht also had a sword which spat sparks that lighted up the country around. This "sword of light" survives as the flaming sword in the crests of O'Flanagan and O'Hart.

So heraldry, a product of the *Respublica Christiana*, associated from its beginings with chivalry—the Church's favoured means of encouraging the observation of an honourable code of behaviour in war—also became in Ireland a means of commemorating our distant, un-Christian past. Despite this reluctance entirely to abandon certain aspects of their pagan culture, the Gaelic Irish embraced the new religion with enthusiasm. In the arms of certain families is the characteristically Gaelic charge of a hand grasping a cross of Calvary. Where this occurs it may denote a family connection with a saint. Such a relationship is certain in the case of the O'Friels who descend collaterally from the same stock as Columbkille. There is also a kinship between that saint and the clan O'Donnell in whose arms there occurs a hand gripping a Passion cross. We have no reason to be so sure of such a link in every instance of its appearance. The arms of McDonnell, where we find a Calvary cross occurring with charges of known pagan origin, present an interesting example of the fusion of two traditions.

Arms and the Diaspora

After the disastrous Battle of Kinsale in 1603 the majority of the native aristocracy tried to conform to the new order. By the process of "surrender and regrant" certain chieftainships were resigned in exchange for peerages, and anciently held septal lands given up to be returned as a grant from the Crown. This was not without personal advantages to the chiefs involved, though much to the detriment of their followers' interests. The new "owner" now had legal title to what had previously been, in Gaelic law, the corporate property of his family. Accepting the English law that now applied to the whole of Ireland involved registration of arms or the seeking of new grants. Those who were unable to accept the new situation, and others who tried initially but also failed to come to terms with the loss, or at least the change in the nature, of their local power left Ireland with some of their followers. The Flight of The Earls in 1607 marks the collapse of the Gaelic culture.

The century that followed saw the accession of a Scottish dynasty to the thrones of the three nations; its expulsion and the period of Parliamentary rule, which in Ireland caused bloody war and massive land confiscation; the restoration of the monarchy and the further change of dynasty from Stuart to Hanoverian. After the final fall of the Stuart cause at Limerick, despite James II's recent unseemly flight from the Battle of the Boyne, his supporters followed him to France where he set up court at St Germain. Some ninety thousand are said to have left after the surrender of Limerick and the total number of Jacobites in France is estimated as having been as high as four hundred and fifty thousand. These included English and Scots though the vast majority were Irish.

Amongst them was James Terry, Athlone Pursuivant of Arms, who took with him his seal of office and heraldic records. Whilst in France he also acquired the famous Book of Lecan (which had apparently been stolen from the library at Trinity College) from a Sir John Fitzgerald for about £100. James Stuart, still regarding himself as King of Scotland, England and Ireland, bestowed honours ranging from peerages to grants of arms and, of course, a herald was needed to record and regulate these matters. In 1690 Terry was appointed Athlone Herald and was able to supply confirmations of arms and details of genealogy to those exiles who chose to serve in the army of France and were obliged to prove their status before being granted commissions. Odd as it may seem to us, he was in correspondence with English and Scots heralds when it was necessary to verify family records and certainly he had access to Irish records such as parish registers and privately held family papers. Even with the thrones of three kingdoms in dispute, there continued a working relationship among the officers of arms of the rival monarchs. Let royal dynasties come and go, heralds proceed with "business as usual."

Terry's surviving letters provide interesting sidelights on the life of the Irish in Europe at the time, and indeed to the trials of his office. It seems that he often found it difficult to get paid for his services, even by his relations, and his letters, though exciting our sympathy, are sometimes very funny. For example, in August 1794 he wrote to the Chevalier Magennis who owed him 50 francs,

> ...I will oblidge you to be as honest man as your father...Dear Knight, Warrior and Cavelier, by all the woden Gods of Greece, I will make you Dance or pay the full Contente of your bill to me....or the Devil shall take you Live...

Even his brother Patrick, who was serving in the Spanish army, sent him nothing for previous professional services ("...and I protest before God it goes hard with me.") when asking for a seal to be made,

> ...lett the armes be without mantling...and a crown atop, a Countes Crown....for in Spain men of my employ have the same honners as a count.

Instead of cash he sent his brother James his assurance that,

> Your punctuality in sending the seal will (in case the time mends) make me think of you oftener...

After the death of Terry Athlone in 1725 the Wild Geese were, ironically, obliged to apply to Ulster King of Arms in Dublin, an appointee of the King of England, for proof of their status as Irish gentlemen.

Anglo-Irish Heraldry

Contemporaneously with the growth and decline of Gaelic armory, the third strain of Irish heraldry had been evolving: the Anglo-Irish. In character it was close to English armory: no longer strictly military and, despite claims of earlier writers on the subject, not always symbolic of family or personal traits and triumphs. Though many would have it that ideally arms should reflect those things, it seems that charges were often chosen quite arbitrarily, but not always. The custom already mentioned, of punning on the family name, continued. Because Gaelic surnames, unlike those of say England or Germany, are seldom the names of objects, such canting arms are not frequently encountered in relation to native Irish names. Perhaps it would be more true to say that they are not as frequently recognised. It may well be that many charges had greater significance for their original users than we now know. Even in languages such as German or French, the archaic forms of which are more accessible to a greater number of people than is medieval Irish, it is often difficult to recognise allusions which, it is felt, must be there. The ancient arms of O'Doherty and Griffin, previously mentioned, are something of a rarity in that they pun an Irish name with an Irish word. An English word used to make a play on an Irish name is found in the arms of Aherne—three herons or hernes. A family of Mullins (a corruption apparently of De Moleyns, not Ó Maoláin) bears a cross *moline*, associating the seemingly Irish name with its Norman French origin. This charge is shared by a family of Molyneaux, though this is less surprising. Certain Anglo-Irish instances of such *armes parlantes* are not too obscure to be spotted by the amateur heraldist. For example, a family of Brooke has for its crest a badger or *broc*. Yet more obvious specimens exist, such as the Kerry family of Gun which bears three cannons.

Though in many cases there was little to distinguish heraldry of this period from English armory other than that the grants were made in Dublin, in others our pagan symbols persist though sometimes, as with the arms of MacSweeney and O'Moroney, O'Cullen and O'Byrne, we find that they are neatly arranged around an ordinary in the English manner. Though these examples refer to Gaelic names and employ Celtic symbols, their manner of arrangement upon the shield places them, in time anyway, as Anglo-Irish. They retain, however, a classic simplicity which was generally lost in English heraldry from Tudor times onward; though that is not to say that the decline in design standards never found its way into Anglo-Irish heraldic art.

It is from this period though that we have many of our most extensive and interesting records. In England heralds had long carried out occasional *Visitations*. Those bearing arms, legally or otherwise, were obliged to have their coats inspected and approved by a visiting herald, who either agreed that they were legitimately borne, made a grant to allow their future use or, rarely, forbade further use of arms entirely. As time went by heralds began to make notes concerning the genealogy of the armigers, some of whom were not above giving themselves a more impressive pedigree than they had in fact. Certain English heralds of the Tudor period are known to have connived with such armigers and in so doing

The arms of O'Byrne: most famous of Celtic symbols disposed on the shield in an English manner.

helped to bring heralds and heraldry into some disrepute.

In Ireland where communications were bad and the geographical extent of English influence a fluctuating thing, it was not practical to carry out visitations until the beginning of the seventeenth century. Even then only three visitations were recorded: in Dublin County in 1606, Dublin City in 1607 and County Wexford in 1618. Unlike England with its College of Arms and a Court of Chivalry to arbitrate upon disputes, Ireland had only the establishment of Ulster King of Arms, though he had the power of the Crown to make decisions in all heraldic matters. This authority was very different from that of any English herald. Because of Ireland's long political fragmentation, its wars and rebellions, heraldic records have never been complete. As a result, Ulster King acquired the power to confirm the right to arms of any who could show their use through three generations, the proof to be provided by the claimant. Norroy and Ulster no doubt retains this power though the procedure is not liked by the Chief Herald's Office.

As compensation for the lack of visitation records in Ireland we have the possibly more useful Funeral Entry Volumes kept by Ulster's office. Records of the great heraldic funerals of notable titled people have left us details of Ulster King's extensive powers and duties in the ordering of ceremonial, and minute accounts of the costs involved. A funeral attended by Officers of Arms; the armiger's peers, family and servants; the mayor of Dublin, his officers and the city's Aldermen, was no mean affair. The funeral of a peer of even moderate rank involved costly embalming, the use of up to 1200 yards of black drapes, large quantities of heraldic painting, the provision of banners, purchase or hire of a hearse, its fitting out in appropriate style, the cost of labour (both men and horses), the feeding and lodging of all involved, all followed by a feast for possibly hundreds of mourners. The provincial gentry were anxious to imitate this show of heraldic pomp and finery, though inevitably upon a reduced scale.

Thomas Preston Ulster's documents list the costs of what he considered to be an extremely modest, even skimped, peerage funeral in the first half of the seventeenth century. The barest necessities, in the way of coats of arms, banners, helmet, sword, velvets, fringes, painting, drapes (hired at a penny per yard), travelling expenses for the officers of arms, livery for their horses at the place of the funeral and, of course, heralds' fees, he estimated,

> The hearse and alter rayles being left out ye charge will be but £59/4/6.

Modest outlay that Preston may have thought it, it still represented many times the annual income of the majority of the population. Even by that time an increasing number of persons of rank were leaving instructions in their wills that large amounts were not to be spent on their funerals. That, plus the increase in popularity of torchlight funerals (a fashion learned from England), led a writer of the time to comment

> that noblemen, and gentlemen of eminent rank are either buried in the night time, with a torch, a two pennie linke, and a lantern; or parsimoniously interred in the day-time by the helpe of some ignorant countrey painter, without the attendance of any of the officers of arms.

So disquieting did Molyneux Ulster find the situation

that he sought and obtained, in 1627, a warrant that ensured the continuation of the system whereby Ulster or his appointed deputies were to attend funerals whether held by torchlight or daylight, oversee heraldic matters, collect fees from armigers' estates and oblige their families to register details of the late armiger's "matches, issues, times of (death) with their armes..." By the same order "painters, masons, glaziers, goldsmiths, cutters, carvers and the like" were charged and commanded that "they presume not to meddle with any matters of armory... without special leave from the King of Arms..." In time Ulster's licenced painters represented him at country funerals, ensuring that emblazonments of arms were accurately executed, that funeral entries were made, fees paid and, not of least importance, that the non-armigerous did not make use of arms without obtaining a proper grant.

The King of Arms' concern with proper procedure at heraldic funerals was primarily in the interest of keeping the Office's records in order, but it was also in his personal interest as all "...buriall clothes as have been for the buriall of any man or woman having armes on them or any other ornaments belonging to his said office..." were for "...him to enjoy the benefit thereof..." This from an Order obtained by Nicholas Narbon Ulster in 1581. Only three years before he had been forced to obtain a similar decree from the Lord Deputy, in which the vicars of Christchurch were forbidden to prevent his removal of such funeral furnishings as were normally his. In the days of civil servants' incomes being derived directly from the revenue their posts produced, all fees went directly to the officers of arms. During the period for which pertinent records survive, 1588—1688, this is estimated to have come to at least £5000. Because fees varied over the years it is difficult to arrive at a precise figure and utterly imposible to estimate quite how much was, in addition, obtained by the right to claim funeral furnishings. One list from a funeral of 1630 amounts to a value of £74/10/8. As may be seen, this would have been a considerable perquisite to the post. One may easily understand how strongly opposed was Ulster to any move by the clergy to usurp the rights of his office.

The problem of collecting fees which James Terry was to encounter in France was no new one. Ulster King's records from earlier the same century have many entries marked, "Fees not paid." With a fine impartiality Gael and Anglo-Irish alike were prosecuted. The class of society most likely to offend in this respect was the titled aristocracy who appear to have made a determined practice of not paying heralds' fees—although one list of defaulters does include a bishop.

The Language of Heraldry

The cross moline, passion and Calvary crosses already mentioned are only three of nearly four hundred varieties of cross known to heraldists, though many of them are extremely rare. Nevertheless it is apparent that any discussion of heraldry calls for the use of some specialised terminology that an ancient tradition has inevitably acquired. The science is rich in fascinating medieval words, many of which are derived from Norman French. Already we have encountered the *field* of a shield, *ordinaries*, *charges*, *crests*, *tincture* and of course *coat armour* and *coat of arms*.

The last term originally applied to the emblazoned surcoat that prevented the heat of the sun falling directly upon a knight's armour. It is often used to apply to the complete *achievement* of arms but strictly means only the shield and what appears on it—the charges. They may be ordinaries which in their most basic form consist of ten arrangements of straight lines, each of which may be *differenced* by being drawn in at least a dozen variations. It can be seen that with the added factor of colour the possible number of variations of even the most simple design runs into many hundreds. Other charges may consist of animals, birds, trees, indeed any object, animate or inanimate, either in nature or the imagination.

Above the shield is the *helm* and falling from it the *mantling* that originally served to keep the sun from the

A complete achievement of arms, that of O'Conor Don,
including shield, helm, crest and supporters. Because of
heraldry's essentially graphic nature the motto is not part of
the achievement—rather, it is a footnote to it. Customarily
the armiger may choose any motto he pleases, though it is
usual in Ireland that the motto, if mentioned in the grant, is
transmitted with the arms.

wearer's neck and possibly to deflect a sword blow. Above the helmet appears the *wreath* of the principal colour and metal of the shield, known heraldically as the *liveries*. On the wreath rests the *crest*. "Crest" is surely the most frequently misapplied heraldic term. It is so often incorrectly used to mean "coat of arms" that it cannot be said too often or too loudly that the two terms are not interchangeable. It is a means of identification quite separate from the shield. At first the crest was a painted design upon the helmet but it later evolved into a three dimensional model which may have been carved from wood or moulded from boiled leather. Sometimes the crest issues from a *coronet of rank* or a *cap of dignity*, though the position of the helmet and its style of visor can also indicate the status of the armiger. While some old grants appear never to have had a crest, a crest is never granted apart from arms.

Supporters, whether human or animal, which bear up the shield, have long been regarded as a mark of honour and from the seventeenth century their use in these islands was restricted to peers and the chiefs of Scottish clans. The single instance of supporters being granted to an Irish Chief of his Name who was not also a peer is the grant made to The O'Conor Don in recognition of his having carried the standard of Ireland at the coronation of Edward VII. Dr MacLysaght, when in office, expressed his willingness to grant supporters to other chiefs but it appears that none have ever applied. There is certainly much to be said for retaining the elegant simplicity of shield and crest without further dressing. It is likely that at first supporters did not indicate the armiger's aristocratic status but were merely a decorative device invented by the engravers of seal matrices who had space to fill between the shield and its circular surround. Their imitation in the design of certain

Gaelic coats, used within the shield to support the principal charge, is probably better discussed in terms of heraldic art, for in the Gaelic context they have no relevance to the rank of the armiger.

The colours, metals and furs of armory are known as tinctures and their names derive mainly from medieval French. They are *argent* (silver), *or*(gold), *gules*(red), *azure* (blue), *sable* (black), *vert*(green), *purpure*(purple), *ermine* and *vair*. Argent is usually painted as white and or as yellow. Ermine is white with black spots. With the colours reversed it becomes *ermines*. The same pattern with black on gold is termed *erminois*, which in reverse is *pean*. Vair is said to represent the skin of a type of squirrel once much used for lining cloaks, blue-grey on the back and white underneath. It is represented in heraldry by a stylised geometrical pattern and unless otherwise stated is always blue and white. Objects described as *proper* are shown in their natural colours.

It might well be asked what is wrong with calling black, red, white or any other colour by its usual name. And the answer is certainly, "Nothing at all". Early writers often used these plain words and there have been those more recently who encouraged such simplification. However, the more esoteric terminology has been so long and so widely used that the heraldist is obliged to know it and finds himself using it, will he, nil he—and it must be admitted that there is a certain satisfaction to be found in its mastery and use. It is all a matter of taste.

At a first encounter this vocabulary may appear obscure and complicated but its rudiments can be learned in an hour and one realizes that it is a precise shorthand for the description of complicated graphic designs. Such a description is known as a *blazon* and allows the experienced heraldist to picture any coat of arms from a

(a)

(b)

(c)

The heraldic furs: (a) Ermine (See "ermines", "erminois" and "paen".) (b) Vair. A field or charge so covered is described as "vairy". (c) Gros vair, also called Counter-vair.

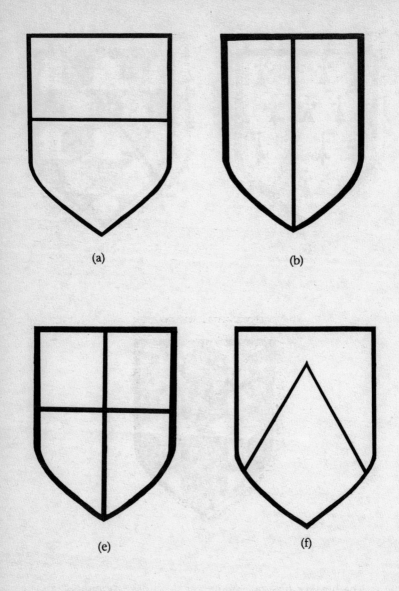

(a)

(b)

(e)

(f)

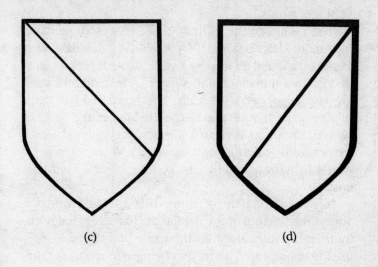

(c)   (d)

(g)

Lines of partition: (a) Per fess, (b) Per pale (c) Per bend, (d) Per bend sinister, (e) Quarterly/Per cross, (f) Per chevron (g) Per saltire.

very few words.

The names of the ordinaries are also used, prefixed by *per*, to describe lines of partition of the field. For example, a shield divided by a vertical line is *per pale*, one divided by a horizontal line is *per fess*. These useful words are also employed to describe the position of charges relative to each other and to the shield's outline. Several objects, say three frogs, in a line across the shield are *in fess*; one atop another they are *in pale*. A sword *fesswise* would be lying across the shield; one *palewise* would be erect.

It is traditional in blazonry that the first word is always the tincture of the field, that charges are followed by their tinctures and that the name of a tincture once used is not repeated, thereafter being referred to as "the field", "the second", "the third", and so on. This fashion for brevity, even at the expense of immediate clarity, originated in the sixteenth century and it is unfortunate that it remains in use, to the confusion of the beginner.

The proper reticence of an early herald in his capacity as an official messenger was far from the exaggerated obscurantism that found its way into all aspects of heraldry during the Tudor period. The many spurious laws and traditions invented at the whim of heraldic writers of that time, and often repeated without thought by their successors, are surely the cause of heraldry having often been regarded as a field of study subscribed to largely by eccentrics. The use of the names of planets and precious stones to indicate colours, and the symbolism attributed to them and to almost every charge, is hardly worth attention. If these practices were known to have been universally adopted by heralds at or after the time of their invention then we could rightly regard arms granted subsequently as examples of symbolic heraldry, even though the symbolism would

(a)

(b)

The repetition of a geometrical charge, such as the fret or the potent, produces an area described as "fretty", as shield (a) or "potenty" as (b).

be somewhat synthetic, but to attempt to apply these principles to earlier armory is nonsense.

The last century and a half has seen a demystification of heraldry and the application of analytical research to its study. It is probably true to say that the subject is nowadays better understood by its enthusiasts than at any time since its heyday in the Middle Ages. However, as a complete understanding depends on the continuous study of earlier documents and commentary, a short dictionary of heraldic terminology follows.

Many possible inclusions have been omitted as being of doubtful value to all but the advanced researcher. These include a number of French and German terms that had their fashionable use at various times, plus others that would only clutter the memory of the reader of this small introduction to the heraldry of Ireland. (For example, it is hard to imagine who would feel it essential to know the correct word to describe a walking tortoise.) For curiosity's sake a few of the more obscure crosses have been included, but little else that is unlikely to be encountered in the blazoning of Irish arms.

It should be mentioned that heraldic spelling is erratic. In blazonry (or blasonry) one meets Escutcheon, Escucheon, Escochon and Scucheon; Affronté, Affrontée and Affronty; Gutté and Gutty; Botoné and Bottony. These and many more Anglicisations of French spelling are a reflection of a similarly debased pronunciation. If French words do not trip easily from your tongue, there is no need to try to make them: it is quite acceptable to rhyme Urdé with Hurdy-gurdy. And there is that irritating little word *or*, so like the conjunction, which catches out even the experienced...

An Heraldic Dictionary

A: In blazonry and the tricking of arms, the abbreviation for argent. Ar is sometimes used but is likely to be mistaken for Az.

Abased or **Abaissé:** Indicates that an ordinary is placed lower on the shield than is usual.

Abatement: A mark of dishonour on an escutcheon, more talked of than actually seen. None is known to exist in Irish or English heraldry though it exists in Scots heraldry.

Achievement: The ensigns upon the shield; the crest; the supporters if any. Often, though not strictly correctly, called the "coat of arms". Does not properly include the motto though slightly different custom prevails in Ireland. See Motto.

Accosted: Side by side.

Accrued: A fully grown tree is said to be Accrued.

Addorsed: Back to back.

Addressed: As Addorsed.

Adumbrated: The shadow of a bearing, outlined and of a colour darker than the field.

Affronty/Affronteé: Facing the front.

Allerion: An eagle lacking legs and beak, displayed.

Antelope: The heraldic antelope dates from a period of poor natural history knowledge and has a beak, serrated horns, tufts on the body and the tail of a lion.

Apaumée: A hand showing the palm. Discussed at some length in the chapter called "Some Gaelic Charges".

Argent: Silver. Usually represented by the use of white.

Armed: When the tincture of a beast's horns, tusks, claws or beak is of a tincture different to that of the body they are said to be Armed of that colour. See Attired.

Alant: A mastiff dog with cropped ears.

Ampyhisian cockatrice: See Basilisk.

Anchor: The heraldic anchor lacks a cable unless stated to have one in the blazon.

Anchored/Ancred: A cross ancred has its extremities shaped like the flukes of an anchor.

Angles: Two angles interlaced, each having an annulet at each end.

Annulet: A ring.

Anshent: Corruption of ancient. A small flag or streamer which may be flown from the back of a ship or from a tent pole. Also applied to the guidon used at heraldic funerals.

Anté/Enté: Grafted, as when one object is inlet to another.

Antique crown: Also called an Antique Irish Crown. A spiked crown, as in the arms of Munster.

Arched/Archy: Bent into the form of an arch.

Arming buckle: A losenge shaped buckle.

Arrondie: Round.

Ascendant: Rising, as smoke, flames or rays of light when issuing upwards.

Aspersed: See Powdered.

Assis: See Sejant.

Asteroids: Stars that resemble planets.

Assurgent: Rising from the sea.

At bay: A stag in its defensive position with bowed head, horns ready to meet adversaries.

Athelstan's cross: An example of arms attributed to a person of pre-heraldic times, King Athelstan of England.

Party per saltire gules and azure, on a bezant, a cross bottony or.

Armiger: A person entitled to bear arms.

At gaze: As guardant but applicable only to deer.

Attired: The antlers of a deer when coloured differently from the body. Also applied by some to the horns of a goat or ram.

Augmentation: An addition to the achievement, usually a mark of honour or commemoration of some special event. If borne upon the shield it is often placed upon an inescutcheon or a canton.

Auré: Dropped with gold.

Avellane: A cross so called because it leaves the exposed quarters of the field shaped like filbert nuts.

Aylet: A chough, sometimes called a sea swallow.

Badge: An heraldic emblem which may or may not be a charge taken from the arms and more likely to be worn by servants than the armiger. Badges are associated with several great English families or individual members of them. In English heraldry the shamrock is a badge of Ireland.

Baillonné: A rarely-used term to describe a rarely-seen charge: a lion rampant with a staff in its mouth.

Ball: This charge is also called a fire-ball and represents a grenade.

Banded: When an object such as a garb of wheat or a bunch of arrows is tied around in a different colour it is said to be banded of that colour.

Banderolle: A narrow flag affixed to a crozier.

Banner: A flag, normally square, charged with the armiger's bearings. Every armiger is entitled to the use of a banner.

Bar: A bar running horizontally across the shield. Similar to the fess but narrower.

Barbed/Barbée: A cross with barbed ends.

Barbed and Crested: See Combed and Wattled.

Bar-gemel: Two narrow bars placed close together.

Baron's coronet: A gold circlet with six pearls.

Barnacle: i) Not the marine creature but the barnacle goose. ii) A blacksmith's tool sometimes found as a charge.

Barrulet: A narrow bar said to be equivalent to a quarter of a normal bar or the twentieth of the field.

Barruly: See Barry.

Barry: When the field is divided into a number of horizontal sections of similar depth it is described as being barry of six, eight, or whatever is applicable. In Irish heraldry it provides the opportunity for the canting arms of the family of Barrett.

Barry-bendy: A shield divided by whatever number of bars, and by the same number of bends (lines from the dexter chief to the sinister base) and the colours of the slanted losenges so formed counterchanged.

Barry-bendy sinister: As above but with bars-sinister, that is, running from the sinister chief to the dexter base.

Barry-indented: Same as Barry-bendy sinister.

Barry-piley: A shield divided by a pile and whatever number of bars stated in the blazon, the colours counterchanged.

Base: The bottom third of the shield.

Basilisk: Same as Cockatrice.

Basnet: A cap worn beneath the helmet in the fourteenth and fifteenth centuries, sometimes appearing as a charge.

Baston: See Baton.

Battled: See Embattled

Battled arrondie: The battlements of a town, circular at the top.

Beaked: When a bird's beak is of a different tincture from the body it is said to be beaked of that colour.

Base: The lower part of the shield.

Baton/Batton/Baston: A staff or truncheon, drawn as a truncated bendlet. Sometimes the baton sinister, "overall" the original coat, denotes illegitimacy.

Bear arms: To display one's coat of arms on appropriate occasions.

Bearing: Any single charge of a coat of arms, though the plural is used to refer to the complete coat.

Bell: A common bell appearing as a charge is blazoned as a Church Bell to avoid confusion with the spherical Hawk's Bell which is so blazoned.

Belled: Wearing bells. Usually applied to hawks, as when blazoned as "jessed and belled."

Bend /Bendlet/Bendy: The bend, an ordinary, is a band running from the dexter chief to the sinister base of the shield and occupying one third of the field if charged or one fifth of it otherwise. A bendlet is half the width of a bend. A field described as bendy is divided bendwise into however many parts indicated in the blazon, i.e. Bendy of six, gules and or.

Bend sinister: A Bend-sinister is as the Bend, but running from the sinister chief to the dexter base. Sometimes but seldom"over-all" as a mark of bastardy.

Besant/Bezant: A gold disc. Discs of other colours have their own names. See Roundels.

Bicapitated: Having two heads.

Bicorporate: Having two bodies attached to one head.

Billet/Billety: This charge is a small rectangle most often found strewn over the whole field, which is then described as Billetty. Should it be repeated fewer than ten times the number must be mentioned in the blazon and their positions specified. Occurs in several Anglo-Irish coats.

Biparted: Cut off to form two points, as opposed to Erased which represents an object, usually a head or a limb, torn off and has three points.

Bladed: Refers to the stalk or blade of any type of corn if of a different tincture from the ear or fruit.

Blazon/Blason: The verbal description of an achievement of arms.

Bordure: A border touching the edge of the shield. Anciently used widely as a mark of difference or distinction and still so used in Scotland.

Botonny/Botoné: See Cross botonny.

Braced: Ordinaries interwoven are described as Braced.

Bretessé: Embattled on both sides, the two matching.

Brisé: See Rompu.

Bristled: See Crined.

Broad arrow: An arrowhead, the insides of the barbs of which are straight. An Irish example of its use is in the arms of Walsh. Sometimes this charge is represented by three narrow triangles. See Pheon.

Bronchant: See Over-all.

Bruske: See Tenné.

Buckles: When used as a charge the shape of a buckle is always stated; i.e. round, square, oval, losenge.

Bugle horn: A hunting horn. When ringed in a different colour it is blazoned as being virolled of that tincture.

Burgundian cross: Two branches in saltire.

Caboshed: The head of an animal affrontée, no part of the neck or body seen, is described as caboshed.

Cadency: Distinction between houses; expressed heraldically by armorial differences.

Caduceus: A winged rod entwined by two serpents.

Caltrap: A charge derived from the four-pointed iron device that was scattered on the ground to impede the passage of cavalry.

Calvary: A Calvary cross is Christ's cross set upon three steps which are sometimes called Grieces.

Camelopard: A giraffe.

Cannet: A duck lacking beak or feet.

Canting arms: Arms which pun on the name of the armiger.

Canton: A small square occupying one third of the chief, normally at the dexter side. Classed as a subordinary.

Caparisoned: Describes a war horse fully equipped for the field.

Cap of maintenance/Cap of dignity: See Chapeau.

Cardinal's hat: The broad brimmed and tasselled hat worn by cardinals appears frequently in ecclesiastical arms.

Cartouche: An oval shield. In the eighteenth and nineteenth centuries it was often surrounded by elaborate decoration.

Castle: See Tower.

Cat-a-mount: A wild cat.

Caterfoil: See Quatrefoil.

Celestial crown: A coronet of eight triangular points, each ensigned with a star.

Cercelée: Describes a cross curling like a ram's horn at its ends.

Chapeau/Cap of Maintenance/Cap of Dignity: An emblem of nobility. This crimson velvet cap, lined and turned up with ermine, sometimes replaces the wreath upon which the crest is rested. In England it is confined to the use of peers but Ulster King of Arms always maintained and exercised a right to grant it to others. An example in Irish armory of its use other than by a peerage family is found in the arms of O'Morchoe.

Chaplet: A garland of flowers and leaves. A chaplet of roses contains only four flowers, the rest leaves.

Charge: Any figure borne upon the field of a shield. When an ordinary or any other charge, a crest or a supporter has another symbol upon it, it is said to be charged with that device.

Chequey: A field or charge composed of equal small squares alternately coloured is described as chequey, chequé or checky.

Chess rook: The heraldic chess rook may not be readily recognisable to the chess player, having a top much like the end of a mill rind.

Chevron: An ordinary like a broad inverted V descending to the extremities of the shield and occupying one fifth of the field. A shield so divided is described as party per chevron. If the field or a portion of it is composed of several chevrons it is chevronny. Chevrons counterpoint stand one upon the head of another. Chevrons couched lie sideways.

Chevronel: The diminutive of the Chevron. Half its width.

Chief: The upper third of the field. A shield so divided is described as *party per chief* and the charges upon the upper portion are *in chief*.

Chief shield: Used to describe a large quartered shield which bears one or more inescutcheons.

Chimaera: A fabulous creature with the head of a lion breathing flames, the body of a goat and the tail of a dragon.

Cinquefoil: A five-leaved figure.

Clarion: An ancient musical instrument which appears as a charge.

Close: The wings of a bird when against the body are described as close, though the term is also used of a helmet with visor down.

Closet: A rarely encountered diminutive of the Bar, half its breadth.

Cockatrice: A fabulous beast having the body and wings of a wyvern but the head of a cock. The supporters of two families of Nugent, including that of the Earls of

Westmeath.

Cognisance: see Badge.

Colours: The colours, metals and furs of heraldry are called tinctures and derive their names mainly from Norman French. (Gules may be of Arabic origin.) They are discussed in the chapter "The Language of Heraldry". Their representation in monochrome is described in "Heraldic Art and Design."

Combatant: Fighting. Said of two figures, most usually lions rampant, placed face to face on a shield.

Combed and Wattled: A cock is said to be combed and wattled of a particular colour if those parts are of a different colour to the body.

Compartment: The area on which supporters stand.

Compony: Divided into oblong shapes of alternating colours. If two rows are used the tinctures are counterchanged and called counter-compony, as in the arms of Doyle which have "a bordure counter-compony or and azure."

Confronty: See Combatant.

Conjoined: Two or more charges joined together are described as conjoined. This word is most frequently met in the phrase "wings conjoined in lure" to describe two wings joined, their tips pointing downwards, as in the arms of Seymour.

Coronet: See section on Crowns and Coronets, and under Duke, Marquis, Earl, Viscount and Baron's Coronets.

Cotised: An ordinary when shown with a narrow diminutive beside it is said to be cotised. With such a band at each side it is Double-cotised.

Couchant: Lying down, head erect.

Counter: In opposition. Most commonly met in the term counterchanged though we also find counter-compony, counter-embattled, counter-embowed, counter-passant, counter-trippant etc.

Counterchanged: A field and charges are said to be counterchanged when the field is party of two tinctures and the charges upon it are of the same; colour placed upon metal, and metal upon colour.

Counter-compony: See Compony.

Countervair: Differs from vair in that the ends of the cup-shaped figures of the same colour are placed against each other, base to base and point to point.

Couped: Shortened, but cut off rather than torn. A cross-couped is cut off so as not to reach the edge of the shield. May be applied to "a head couped at the neck", "a hand couped at the wrist" etc. A head close-couped would be cut off at the top of the neck rather than the base.

Courant: Running.

Cowed: With the tail between the legs.

Crampon: An iron device for fixing stones together. When used as a charge its ends are hooped.

Cramponée: A cross-cramponée has a square cramp at each end.

Crenellée: Embattled.

Crescent: Half moon with its points towards the top of the shield.

Crest: The figure appearing above the wreath, coronet or chapeau, on top of the helmet.

Cri-de-geurre: A war cry. Sometimes used as a motto but may appear in addition to the motto, placed above the shield.

Crined: Said of hair when of a different tincture to the body.

Cronal: The multi-pointed tip of a jousting lance.

Cross: An ordinary formed by intersecting two vertical parallel lines with two horizontal parallel lines at about the fess-point. Should the ends of the lines be shortened so as not to reach the perimeter of the shield it is termed a cross-couped. If the lines are drawn to intersect visibly it is termed a cross quarter-pierced. Otherwise it is a cross. Uncharged it occupies one fifth of the field; if charged, one third. The many variations of the cross in heraldry are a study in their own right. The more common ones are mentioned in this glossary, though one or two rarities are listed for the sake of the curious.

Crosslet: A cross-crosslet has a cross at each of its extremities.

Crosswise: Several charges, usually five, placed in the form of a cross.

Crozier: A bishop's staff.

Crusuly: Strewn with crosses.

Cubit arm: A hand and arm couped at the elbow.

Damasked: See Diapered.

Dancetty: Large indenting of more than three points.

Debruised: A single charge obscured by an ordinary is described as debruised. If more of the coat is covered the blazon would read,"over all" a bar, baton, bend etc.

Decrescent: The moon in its last quarter, its points toward the sinister side of the shield.

Deer's attires: The antlers of a deer.

Defamed: An animal defamed lacks its tail.

Degraded: A cross degraded has steps at each end.

Demi- : Half, as in demi-lion, demi-vol, demi-fleur-de-lis.

Dexter: The right hand side of the shield as carried, not as seen. Anything in heraldry belonging to the right, e.g. a supporter, the male side of an impaled coat, is referred to as the dexter. Unless otherwise stated, animals and other figures are assumed to be facing the dexter side.

Diadem: An early form of crown, probably derived from a head-band.

Diapered/Damasked: The field of a shield when

decorated with patterns of a lighter or darker shade of the tincture of the field is described as diapered or damasked. Abstract figures such as arabesques are used to avoid these decorative devices being mistaken for charges. Fine examples of diapering can be seen in the armorial stained glass at the Royal Hospital, Kilmainham.

Difference: The changes to a shield, whether extra charges or a change of tincture, which distinguish one branch of a family from another. See Distinction.

Diminutives: All ordinaries have a diminutive form. The Pale's diminutive is the pallet. The Bend has the bendlet. The Bar has the barrulet, closet and bar gemel. The Chevron has the chevronel. The Bordure's diminutives are the orle and the tressure.

Dimidation: An early and somewhat inelegant form of impalement which divided the two shields in pale and joined the dexter of the male shield to the sinister of the female.

Disarmed: A creature lacking its natural weapons, i.e. claws, beak etc., is described as Disarmed.

Displayed: A bird with fully open wings is described as displayed. As in the arms of O'Boylan, O'Moriarty, Browne and others.

Distilling: Dripping, usually blood.

Distinction: When differences are mentioned in the blazon as being "for distinction" they indicate either that there is no blood relationship to persons bearing similar arms, or bastardy.

Dormant: Sleeping, the head resting on the forepaws.

Double-queued: Having two tails. See Queue forchée.

Double tressure: See Tressure.

Dovetail: Any ordinary or line of partition drawn to resemble the carpenter's dove-tailed joint.

Ducal coronet: This coronet, called in Ireland a "ducal crest coronet", is not a coronet of rank. It is no longer granted but its use continues in arms granted at an earlier period. It has four strawberry leaves set around its rim, three of them visible. Not to be confused with a duke's coronet which has eight, five visible.

Eagle: A common charge in the heraldry of all nations, often said to denote imperial status, but not so in Irish heraldry.

Earl's coronet: This coronet has above the rim eight pyramidal points, each surmounted by a pearl, and below eight strawberry leaves placed alternately.

Eastern crown: A plain rim with triangular spikes. This is not a mark of rank, though doubtless some armigers would like it to be mistaken for such. For this reason it is not nowadays readily granted.

Embowed: An arm from the shoulder, bent at the elbow, is described as embowed.

Eft: See Evet.

Embattled/Imbattled/Crenelée: Like the battlements of a tower. Also a line of partition.

Embrued: Bloody. Usually said of an edged weapon.

Endorsed/Addorsed: Back to back.

Enfield: A fabulous creature with the head of a fox, the chest of a greyhound, fore-legs as the legs of an eagle, body of a lion and the hind-legs and tail of a wolf. Not seen other than as the crest of some families of Kelly.

Enfiled: A sword enfiled has a severed head upon it. The crest of Clancy provides an Irish specimen.

Engrailed: An ordinary having outward facing points formed by semi-circles is described as engrailed. See Invected.

Ensigned: A charge described as ensigned is borne upon another. An Irish example is the arms of Gavan, the principal charge of which is a sword ensigned by a mullet.

Erased: Torn off so as to leave the erased object with a ragged edge.

Eradicated: Said of a tree or other plant torn up by the roots, as in the arms of Donnellan, Boyle and Hegarty.

Ermine: A fur, white with black spots.

Ermines: A fur, black with white spots.

Erminois: A fur, gold with black spots.

Escarbuncle: A wheel with eight spokes sometimes terminating in fleurs-de-lis. This charge probably originated as the metal boss of a shield.

Escutcheon: A shield. A small shield borne as a charge is termed an Inescutcheon, commonly found as an escutcheon of pretence bearing the arms of the armiger's father-in-law (after death) indicating that the bearer holds some of his property by his marriage to an heiress.

Estoile: A star with six wavy points. If there are more than six points the number must be stated in the blazon. See Mullet.

Evet: A lizard.

Falchion: A type of broadsword.

Falcon: Falcons occur in the armory of all countries but in Ireland are associated particularly with several Tipperary families.

Fess: An ordinary. A horizontal band on the shield occupying one third of the field.

Fess point: The approximate centre of the escutcheon.

Fesswise: Any charge borne Fesswise is placed horizontally on the shield.

Field: The surface of the shield bearing the charge or charges. It is always the first thing mentioned in the blazon.

Fimbriated: A cross having a narrow border of another tincture is said to be fimbriated.

Fitchée/Fitchy/Fiched: Said of a cross with its lower point sharpened.

Flaunches/Flanches: Curved lines running from the

upper corners of the shield to the base points. Flanches are never borne singly but always one each side of the shield. The outside areas which they define are known as the flanks of the shield.

Fleur-de-lis: Stylised representation of a lily associated with the kings of France but not reserved to their use. It occurs in the arms of several Irish families such as those of Dolan and Nowlan.

Fleury-counterfleury: Applies to an ordinary having alternating demi fleur-de-lis on its outer sides.

Flexed: Bent.

Flighted: The feathers of an arrow when coloured differently from the shaft are said to be flighted of that tincture.

Flory/Fleury: Decorated with one or more fleur-de-lis. A cross Fleury terminates in fleurs-de-lis.

Flotant: Flying in the air, as a banner flotant.

Formée/Pattée: A cross very small at the centre and broadening towards its extremities is termed cross patée or formée.

Fountain: A roundel barry wavey, usually of six, argent and azure.

Fourcée: Forked or divided, as queue forchée.

Fret: A mascel and saltire interlaced, as in the arms of the Anglo-Irish family of Vernon and the Norman family of Blake. A field or charge entirely covered with interlaced bendlets and bendlets-sinister is described as fretty, as in the arms of McCann.

Fructed: A tree bearing fruit is said to be fructed.

Furnished: See Caparisoned.

Furs: See Ermine, Erminois, Ermines, Paen, Vair.

Fusil: An elongated losenge.

Gamb: See Jamb.

Garb: A sheaf of wheat or other corn, as in the arms of Fogarty and Cummins. In the arms of Cummins they are sometimes blazoned as "garbs of cumin"; in the arms of Otley as "garbs of oats". The Anglo-Irish family of Hatton, like many families originating in Cheshire, bear garbs which were chosen in imitation of the anciently recorded bearings of the Earls of Chester.

Gardant/Guardant: Animals facing the viewer of the shield are Gardant.

Garnished: Ornamented.

Gemmells: See Bar gemell.

Ghibelline battlements: Dovetailed castellations.

Gobony: See Componée.

Golp: A purple roundel.

Gorge: See Whirlpool.

Gorged: Collared. When the collar is of a different colour from the animal it is blazoned as being gorged of that tincture.

Goutty/Goutée: A field or charge strewn with drops is goutty. Goutty de sange denotes drops of blood.

Grieces: The steps, usually three, which support a Calvary cross.

Griffin: A monster the front of which approximates to the body of an eagle but has large ears, while the trunk and hind quarters of the body are those of a lion. The male griffin, we are told, has no wings. Sometimes, as in the arms of Ryan, the head only is used.

Gross vair: See Countervair.

Guardant: see Gardant.

Gules: Red.

Gutée: See Goutty.

Gyron: A triangular figure, usually a half of a quarter, almost always appearing in the dexter chief.

Gyronny: A field gyronny is divided into eight triangular parts, alternately tinctured. Rarely the blazon will state, gyronny of six, ten or twelve.

Harpy: A monster having the head and bust of a

woman and the wings and body of a vulture.

Hatching: The standard system of indicating the colours of heraldic achievements in monochrome. See the chapter, "Heraldic Art and Design."

Hatchment: A corruption of "achievement." Used to describe the display of the arms of a dead person. Usually the escutcheon is set upon a background of a black losenge and hung on the front door of the deceased armiger's house during the period of mourning. This form of display is now little used.

Haurient: Fishes placed upon the shield palewise are said to be haurient.

Hawk: A bird blazoned as a hawk may be depicted as either a true hawk or as a falcon unless the species is stated. A hawk's bell is spherical and quite unlike a church bell. A hawk's lure is the dummy bird used to recall the hawk to the falconer and is represented by an object similar to wings conjoined in lure, though usually with a cord attached. This charge appears in the arms of the Anglo-Irish families of Jebb and Falkiner.

Hay-fork: Sometimes called a shakefork, this bearing may be described heraldically as "a pale couped, forked and pointed." It looks much like a letter Y and should not be confused with an archbishop's pall. It appears in the arms of several families of Conyngham/Cunningham, including those of the Marquis of Slane.

Helmet/Helm: The helmet is an essential part of the achievement. Its position and the type and position of the visor may indicate the status of the armiger. See the chapter "The Helmet and the Crest".

Herald: See the chapter, "The Office of Herald."

Hexagram: Two equilateral triangles interlaced, one of them inverted, forming a six-pointed star. Otherwise known as the Star of David.

Honour point: The point directly above the centre of

the shield.

Hurt: A blue roundel.

Imbattled: See Embattled.

Impale: To join two complete coats of arms palewise on a marriage. The lady's arms are placed on the sinister.

Increscent: A crescent moon with its points to the dexter side.

Indented: A line of partition similar to dancetée though with smaller teeth and no limit to the number used.

Inescutcheon: See Escutcheon.

Invected: A line of partition similar to engrailed but the teeth turning inward.

Inverted: Any charge blazoned as inverted is placed the wrong way up. Wings inverted are shown with the points down.

Irradiated: With rays of light issuing from it.

Issuant: A charge coming out of a line or border is said to be issuant from it. If blazoned simply as Issuant it is understood to be coming out of the bottom of the chief.

Jamb: The fore-leg of an animal. If couped or erased in the middle joint it becomes a paw.

Jessant: Springing forth. Applied to vegetables of which only the upper half may be seen.

Jessed: A hawk jessed is wearing leather restraining straps on its legs.

Label: A mark of difference which, depending on whether or how it is charged, indicates degrees of cadency. See section of main text on differencing.

Lambrequin: Mantling.

Langued: The tongue of a beast is always gules except when the beast itself is so tinctured, in which case it is langued azure; or when the blazon states it to be langued of another colour or metal.

Leash: i) The leather thong for restraining a hawk or hound. ii) Three of anything, as a leash of hares.

Leopard: This creature is seldom seen entire in modern heraldry though in earlier times that was not so. A lion passant gardant such as the three lions of England which were originally termed leopards. More recently only the head of the leopard is shown. If couped or erased at the neck it is blazoned as a leopard's head. If it is caboshed it is known as a leopard's face.

Lined: The lining of a mantle or cloak when used heraldically is said to be lined of a particular tincture, often a fur.

Lines of partition: Any line the shape of any ordinary used to divide the shield is a line of partition. See illustration of ordinaries and lines of partition.

Lion: An extremely common charge which occurs in Irish heraldry of all periods. Unless otherwise stated it is assumed to be rampant. If gules it may be assumed to be armed and langued azure unless otherwise stated.

Liveries: The principal tinctures of the shield are called the livery colours or liveries.

Lodged: Couchant, but only applied to deer.

Losenge: A rhombus standing upon its point. The arms of a lady are usually, but not always, borne upon a losenge.

Losengy: A field or charge bendy-bendy sinister, tinctures counterchanged, is termed losengy.

Lymphad: An ancient singl-masted ship with sail and oars, often shown with both in use.

Maltese cross: This cross, its four limbs of equal length and narrow at the inner ends, broad and bi-pointed at the extremities, is so called because it is borne by the members of the Order of Malta.

Mantling: The piece of cloth attached to the helmet, originally used to prevent the sun falling directly on the wearer's neck. Heraldically it is usually of the liveries.

Marquis's coronet: A circlet of gold with four strawberry leaves around its rim, interspersed with four spikes ensigned with pearls.

Marshal: To join together two or more coats of arms, including augmentations and other entitlements of the armiger. Part of the work of the herald.

Martlet: A house martin or swallow lacking feet. Used as a mark of difference on the shield of a fourth son.

Mascle: A voided losenge.

Masoned: A building with its mortar a different colour from the stonework is said to be masoned of that tincture.

Maunch: A sleeve of a lady's dress.

Membered: The beak and legs of a bird when a different colour from that of the body may be said to be membered of that tincture.

Mill-rind: The metal centrepiece of a millstone. shaped like an elongated X, its extremities pointed and curved outwards, pierced at the centre.

Moline: A cross with its ends like a mill rind. A common charge but also used as a difference for the arms of an eighth son.

Mount: A hillock, usually blazoned vert.

Mound: See Orb.

Mullet: Often mistaken for a star but in fact the rowel of a spur with five points.

Mural crown: An embattled crown.

Murrey: Dark red. A rare heraldic tincture.

Naiant: Swimming.

Naissant: One charge which appears to be coming out of an ordinary or other charge.

Naval crown: A coronet composed of the sterns and sails of ships.

Nebuly/Nebulée: A line of partition said to resemble clouds but more like a line of arches, narrow at the base and widening toward their tops.

Nimbus: A halo.

Nombril point: A point on the escutcheon directly below the fess point.

Nowed: Knotted. Often applied to snakes, as in the crest of Cavendish.

Octofoil: Eight-leaved.

Ombrello: An umbrella, most often found in ecclesiastical arms as a mark of dignity.

Or: Gold, usually represented by the use of yellow.

Orb: A piece of royal regalia, one of the emblems of kingship, consisting of a ball ensigned with a cross.

Ordinaries: The most basic geometrical charges are known as Ordinaries or the Honourable Ordinaries. See section in main text.

Orle: A border within the shield but not touching its edges. In-orle describes a number of charges, usually eight, arranged around the escutcheon along the line an orle would occupy. In-orle may also be used of two objects, such as branches, describing an arch shape.

Ostrich: The heraldic ostrich is depicted as the natural one but often with a metal object in its beak, nearly always a horseshoe. An Irish example is the arms of MacMahon of Oriel.

Over all: A charge obscuring other charges is blazoned as over-all. See Debruised.

Pale: An ordinary. A vertical band down the centre of the escutcheon and occupying one third of the field.

Paley: A field or charge the surface of which is covered in pales of alternating tinctures.

Palisado crown: A coronet of palisades or stakes pointed at the top. Not a coronet of rank. See Vallery.

Pallet: A diminutive of the pale, half its width.

Pall/Pallium: A piece of ecclesiastical regalia. Shaped like a letter Y reaching the dexter and sinister chief points of the shield and usually fringed at the lower extremity.

Panther: The heraldic panther is always gardant. Sometimes it has flames isuing from the mouth and is blazoned as "a panther incensed."

Parted: Divided into segments.

Partition lines: See Lines of partition.

Party: A divided field is described as party per fess, per bend, etc.

Passant: Walking.

Passion cross: The cross of Christ.

Patée: A cross patée broadens considerably towards its extremities. When blazoned "a cross patée throughout" or "a cross patée entire" it reaches the edges of the field.

Patriarchal cross: A cross with two crossbars, the lower being the longer.

Pean: A fur, black with gold ermine spots.

Pelican: The heraldic pelican is often shown "vulning herself" or blazoned as "a pelican in her piety". Legend has it that the female pelican draws blood from her breast to feed her young. As the crest of Aherne.

Pellet: A black roundel, also known as a gunstone or, rarely, an ogress.

Pennon: A small flag narrowing to one or two points, attached to a lance end.

Per bend/Per chevron/Per pale etc. : See Party.

Per cross: A field divided per cross has quarters of two or more tinctures uncharged. If charged they are blazoned as quarterly.

Pheon: An arrowhead with the inside of the barbs curved. If it has its point upwards it should be blazoned as "inverted." See Broad arrow.

Phoenix: The phoenix is represented in just the same way as "a demi-eagle displayed" but issuing from flames.

Pierced: An ordinary blazoned as pierced has a hole through it enabling the field to be seen.

Pile: An ordinary consisting of a wedge shape emerging from the chief.

Plate: A silver roundel.

Plume: Feathers "in plume" consist of a bunch of three feathers unless blazoned otherwise, e.g. a plume of five ostrich feathers, as in the crest of Butler.

Pomeis: A green roundel.

Pomée: A cross pomée has a ball at each extremity.

Popinjay: A parrot.

Potent: A cross potent has T-shaped ends and is so called because of its resemblance to a crutch, anciently called a potent.

Potenty: A field composed entirely of potents is potenty. Counter-potenty indicates that the broad ends of the same colour are placed together.

Powdered: Strewn. A field bearing the same charge repeated many times is said to be powdered of that charge.

Pretence: See Escutcheon of pretence. Also applied to arms related to particular property to which the armiger no longer has title. The inclusion of the Irish harp in the arms of Great Britain is an example of pretence.

Pride: A peacock in its pride has its tail full extended. An Irish example is the crest of Comerford.

Proper: A charge blazoned as proper is shown in its natural colours.

Purpure: Purple. A seldom-used tincture.

Quarter: As a sub-ordinary, a quarter of the shield. However, a shield described as quarterly may contain arms to which the armiger is entitled by marriage. Certain Gaelic shields are quartered, but for purposes of design rather than marshalling. See main body of text.

Quatrefoil: A four-leaved figure.

Quintuple mount: Two mounts resting upon three mounts.

Raguly: A line of partition, like battlements slanting towards the dexter.

Rampant: Rearing up.

Rayonant: A cross rayonant has rays of glory behind it, originating at its centre and reaching the edges of the shield.

Rayonée: A line of partition like tongues of flame is said to be rayonée.

Reclinant: Bending backwards.

Reguardant: Looking backward.

Renversé: Any charge inverted is renversé. Also said of a beast lying on its back.

Respectant: Two figures facing each other, but not combatant, are respectant.

Reversed: Figures contrary to each other or anything contrary to the usual position.

Rising: A bird with its wings half open, as when about to fly, is said to be rising.

Rompu: A broken ordinary, particularly a chevron, is said to be rompu.

Rose: An heraldic rose has five petals. It should be blazoned as "barbed vert"and "seeded or" though it is seldom seen any other way. If the stem is seen it is "slipped and leaved."

Roundel: A disc. See Bezant, Golp, Hurt, Plate, Pomei, Tortaeu, Pellet.

Rustre: A losenge pierced with a round hole.

Sable: Black.

Salade/Sallet: A helmet with a broad brim.

Salient: Leaping.

Saltire: An ordinary formed by crossing the bend and the bend- sinister, occupying one fifth of the field if uncharged and one third if charged.

Sanguine: Blood red.

Scarpe: A diminutive of the bend-sinister.

Scroll: The strip containing the motto.

Scutcheon: See Escutcheon.

Sea- : The prefix sea- indicates that the creature has the lower body of a fish, e.g. sea-lion, sea-dog etc.

Seax: A scymitar with a small semi-circle cut from the back of the blade.

Segreant: Said of a griffin erect on its hind legs, the wings indorsed and displayed as about to fly.

Sejant: Sitting.

Semy: Strewn irregularly over the field, e.g. semy of fleur-de-lis.

Sextuple mount: A mount set upon two mounts set upon three.

Shakefork: see Hayfork.

Shamrock: A green trefoil, a badge of Ireland but not our national emblem which is the harp. See the chapter "National and Provincial Arms."

Sinister: The left of the shield, as carried not as seen. Anything belonging to the left, on the field or outside the shield, is blazoned as sinister.

Slip: The stem of a plant or flower, when coloured differently from the flower, is said to be slipped of that tincture.

Spiked mace: This weapon is so blazoned to distinguish it from a civic mace.

Splendour: The sun in his splendour has a human face and emits rays from around its perimeter. An Irish example is found in the arms of Brady.

Springing: As salient but applied to beasts of the chase.

Stains: Rarely-used mixed colours: sanguine, murrey, tenné.

Standard: A narrow flag bearing arms, crest and badges if any.

Stars: See Estoile and Mullet.

Statant: Standing.

Sub-ordinaries: The border, orle, inescutcheon, quarter, canton, billet, pall, pile, flaunche, losenge, mascle, fusil, roundel, and fret are the sub-ordinaries; to which some would add those fields and (rare) charges which are chequey, fretty, potenty, losengy and goutté.

Sun: See Splendour.

Supporters: Figure, human or animal, standing outside the shield and bearing it up. The area upon which they stand is the compartment.

Surmounted: A bearing placed over or upon another.

Syren: A mermaid.

Talbot: A large scent-hound.

Tau cross: Otherwise "St Anthony's Cross", much like a letter T curving and widening towards its extremities.

Tawny/Tenné: A seldom used colour, brownish orange.

Throughout: Used to describe a charge touching the sides of the shield which does not normally do so.

Tierced/Tiercé: A shield divided into three equal parts of different tinctures is tiercé.

Tincture: A colour, metal or fur used in armory.

Torteau: A red roundel.

Tower: It is important to note that a tower and a castle are not the same charge. A tower has no supprting walls, as in the arms of Kelly, Plunket, Egan, O'Higgins and many other Irish families, while a castle, of however many towers, has walls between them, as in the arms of the City of Limerick or the Norman family of Redmond.

Towered: Surmounted by one or more towers, as in the arms of Kelly, "a tower triple towered."

Trefoil: A three-leaved figure, usually slipped.

Trick of arms: A monochrome representation of an achievement of arms, the tinctures indicated by the following abreviations: A: Argent, Az: Azure, Vt: Vert, Sa: Sable, Gu: Red, Or: Gold. Purp: Purpure.

Triple mount: A mount set upon two mounts.

Trippant/Tripping: As passant but applied to beasts of the chase, as in the arms of Hennessy, McCarthy, O'Connell, O'Sullivan and many more Irish families. Counter-trippant refers to two beasts passing in opposite directions.

Trussing: A hawk upon its prey is said to be trussing it, as in the arms of Madden.

Turreted: Having small turrets, as upon a wall or tower.

Tyger/Tiger: The heraldic tiger is not readily recognisable to the naturalist, having a body more or less like that of the real animal, a lion's mane and tufted tail, and a head much like that of the antelope. A natural tiger is blazoned as a Bengal tiger.

Undée: Waved.

Unguled: Used of the feet of ungulates when of a different colour from the body.

Unicorn: The unicorn is not merely a horse with a horn, but has the body of an antelope, the tail of a lion and a bearded horse's head with a single horn.

Urdée: An ordinary so widely perforated that only its edges are visible is decribed as urdée.

Urinant: A fish palewise, head to the chief.

Vair: A fur, always blue and white unless otherwise stated in the blazon. See illustration in main text. A field or charge so covered is vairy.

Visor: The position and type of an helmet's visor denotes the status of the armiger. See chapter "The Helmet and the Crest."

Vallerry: A crown vallery or vallery coronet is not a mark of rank. Much like the palisado crown but with fewer and broader ascenders.

Vambraced: An arm in armour may be described as Vambraced. Extremely common as part of a crest.

Varvels: Small rings attached to the ends of a hawk's jesses.

Vert: Green.

Virroled: The ornamental bands of a hunting horn. Virrols when tinctured differently from the horn itself are described as virroled of that colour.

Voided: The centre of an ordinary cut away to reveal the colour of the field, leaving a border.

Vol: Wings conjoined in lure.

Volant: Flying.

Vorant: A beast swallowing another.

Vulned: Wounded.

Water bouget: a stylised representation of two water bags hanging from a yoke. A rare Irish example is seen in the arms of a family of Hunt.

Wattled: See Barbed and wattled.

Wavy: A line of partition resembling waves.

Wreath: The twisted cloth which surmounts the helmet providing a seat for the crest. Usually of the liveries.

Wyvern: A dragon having a serpentine tail rather than hind legs.

Yale: A spotted, goat-like monster with boar's teeth and a unicorn's feet.

Zebra: Not found in Irish heraldry but worth inclusion as an example of modern symbolic heraldry. Used as supporters to the arms of Botswana, representing co-operation between the country's black and white citizens.

The Helmet and The Crest

It has been mentioned earlier that the position of the helmet and the type or position of its visor can denote the status of the armiger. This convention is a creation of the Stuart period when full armour was no longer used and heraldry, being less of a necessity on the battlefield, was in something of a decline. The social value of being the possessor of a coat of arms was more in mind than armory's strictly practical origin and the enhancement of the éclat attached to arms drove other considerations into second place. Briefly, the helm of a gentleman or esquire is of steel and shown in profile, its visor closed; that of a knight or baronet is open and affronté; a peer's is silver, grilled, and seen in profile; a royal helmet is gold, grilled, and affronté. These rules are still applied in Northern Ireland but as no such scale of ranks any longer exists in the Republic are here somewhat obsolete. The majority of Irish armigers would use the first. Southern citizens who bear titles originating in earlier times doubtless display their helmets as represented on their grants. These regulations of late invention are of strictly English origin, being unknown in continental Europe. Even in Britain they are disliked by many heraldists and damned by being termed "paper heraldry", which is to say that they have no relevance to the original function of armory nor even any basis in a tradition of ancient use to commend them.

When helmets resembling those depicted in heraldry

were worn on the battlefield or for the tourney, what was worn by whom was a matter dictated by the style of the time and the taste of the wearer. Patterns of helmet changed considerably over the centuries and it is perfectly proper for any type of full-faced helmet to be used heraldically, though it is probably best to avoid infringing the rules mentioned above, no matter how unnecessary one feels them to be. Bearing in mind that the crest as we know it was probably a decoration belonging to the tournament helmet rather than that worn in battle, it may be more appropriate to use the jousting helm in heraldic representations. As a knight was awarded more points for striking his opponent's helmet than elsewhere, this piece of equipment was large, heavy and by no means suitable for use throughout a full day of fighting. At the tournament it was either carried by a page or slung from the saddle until needed, only being placed on the head at the latest possible time.

Very few helmets have survived. Considering how many thousands of them must have been in existence this is surprising; though probably then as now, out-of-date military equipment was of little value and not thought worth preserving. One would not think this of those more elaborate ones which we have from the period during which they were made for ceremonial purposes and not actually worn. Then practicality gave way to elegance and they are often of such a shape that their wearing is impossible. Unfortunately it is from these that many of the heraldic artists of later times took their pattern.

From the top of the helmet appends the mantling or lambrequin. It has been variously theorised that this piece of fabric is purely decorative; that it was worn to help deflect a sword blow; that it served to keep the sun from falling directly upon the metal helmet. The last of these seems the most popular explanation though the second seems likely also. That it provided an opportunity for decoration is certain. Heraldic artists have represented it in all possible forms, from a mere duster to the most elaborate "bed of seaweed" style of the eighteenth and nineteenth century, a feathery, damascened confection entirely surrounding the rest of the achievement. The transition between the two was by way of the wish to represent a knight's mantling as slit and torn by sword cuts.

In early grants the colours of the mantling were usually the liveries. At a later stage argent and gules became fashionable and remained so for some centuries. Arms originating during that period continue to be represented so, but in modern grants they are always of the principal tinctures of the arms. At various times in other countries the mantling has been scattered with charges, has become a fur-lined cloak, has grown to a representation of a royal tent, and the Grand Falconer to the kings of France had two hawk's lures hanging from his.

Atop the helmet is placed a coronet of rank, a cap of dignity or, most commonly, the wreath or torse, which provides a seat for the crest. Many of the wide range of objects used as crests would not rest securely on a helmet without some form of padding and the wreath represents twisted cloths of the livery colours.

In all probability the crest of helmets worn in battle was often a fixed part of the helmet of the fan shape seen in many old drawings. This would have prevented a sword blow being taken directly on the head. Painting of helmets was common and this fan would have provided another surface on which to show the knight's emblems. The huge crests of carved wood or moulded leather seen on ceremonial helmets would have been utterly impractical in battle and even in the tourney. Though such ornaments made a fine show for ceremonial purposes, they could hardly have been suitable wear for even a short bout of jousting. Some old achievements were depicted without a crest. Some are known to have had crests added at a later date. This has been accounted for by the fact that not all armigers were eligible to compete in tournaments, even though liable for military service. Those ineligible would have had no need for elaborate crests to their helmets. In later times, when jousting was no longer practised and tournament status a thing of the past, crests may have been adopted and subsequently confirmed to the use of the armiger. Nowadays arms are seldom granted without a crest (in England, never) though one recent instance is worth note: the coat of the late ex-President Sean T. O'Kelly, as exemplified on his plate in the National Heraldic Museum, has no crest.

The frequent confusion of the terms "crest" and "coat of arms" has already been mentioned. This common error is at least in part the result of the eighteenth and nineteenth century fashion for engraving just the crest, rather than the complete achievement, on silverware, jewelry and writing paper. A certain type of tradesman was ever willing to turn a coin out of his customers' snobbery and ignorance. A "family crest" could be found for anybody who did not care to enquire too closely into what authority the jeweller or stationer had for attributing this or that emblem to the client. For a period of at least a century stationers seem to have created as many armigers as did heralds—and the practice continues.

Unlike the shield, a crest may be shared by several unrelated families. It is, therefore, clear that without the supporting evidence of the rest of the achievement, the crest is an inadequate means of identification. There are however certain crests associated with particular Irish names which would never be granted to a petitioner not known to be related to that armigerous family. For example, the enfield, a fabulous creature described as having the head of a fox, the chest of a greyhound, talons of an eagle, body of a lion and hind legs and tail of a wolf, is peculiar to the O'Kellys of Hy Many and its use by a Kelly that cannot prove a relationship to that sept is unlikely to be allowed. Neither the crest of O'More which includes a sword pierced through three gory heads, nor that of Sheene (an arm in armour embowed, hand proper, holding aloft a severed head) is likely to have a rush of petitioners anxious to share it. There are numerous variations of hands holding edged weapons in the crests of Irish and Scots armory of the Gaelic school. Even armoured hands, though a late introduction, should not be dismissed as un-Gaelic because they wear armour untypical of that used by the Gael. They certainly represent a continuation of the earlier hand-symbol tradition.

Amongst our Irish families of Norman descent are further examples of crests that instantly name the bearer for us. The use of the ape of the Fitzgeralds (whether or not such an animal ever in fact rescued one of the name from danger as the legend has it) may be said to be the sole right, in Ireland, of that family. The falcon rising from amongst ostrich feathers will always be associated with various branches of the Butlers. A stag with a crucifix between its antlers is the crest of families of Eustace and Power and recalls the story of St Hubert, patron of hunters, who met a deer so adorned whilst hunting in a forest. After this he founded a monastery and devoted his life to pious practices, though he continued to hunt and to breed hounds which were the progenitors of our modern bloodhounds and foxhounds. One cannot help but wonder whether here we have another example of the anciently sacred being adopted into Christian mythology.

These examples from Gaelic and Norman heraldry can be matched by a few just as distinctive from the Anglo-Irish school. While many are shared by other Anglo-Irish and English families, some are certainly appropriate to the name, such as that of a family of Banner: an arm in armour, embowed, in hand a banner charged with a fleur-de-lis (the principal charge of the shield). Others are distinctive if only as examples of the decline in the standard of heraldic design in the post-Tudor period. Paper heraldry, arms both Gaelic and Anglo-Irish which were never intended for the battlefield, allowed the use of objects for crests which could never in fact have been fixed upon a helmet. "MacGillycuddy's Reeks proper" cannot be considered to be truly heraldic in character. The crest of Fiddes is a more extreme example of poor heraldic taste: a cornucopia standing upon its point and saved from accidents by being grasped by two hands which issue from clouds! There is one example, the crest of a family of Keane from Waterford, which, despite their Gaelic name (Ó Céin) and the choice of a Gaelic charge (three salmon) suggests that the original armiger, like many native Irishmen of the period, saw his country's interests best served by the political link with Britain. It is a cat-a-mount holding in its paw a Union flag.

Caps, Coronets and Crowns

A Cap of Dignity, also called a Cap of Maintenance and a Chapeau, was a scarlet cap lined and turned up ermine, worn by noblemen of the Middle Ages. Sometimes it replaces the wreath as a foundation for the crest and as such is probably reminiscent of the "capelot" once worn on top of an actual helmet and from which the mantling developed. In England and Wales its use is said to be limited to peers, though its granting outside of the peerage is known from Stuart times. In Scotland and Ireland, however, the Lord Lyon and Ulster King of Arms have always claimed and maintained a right to grant it to whom they may think fit. There are several Irish instances of its use by armigers other than members of the peerage. The O'Morchoe, Chief of his Name, bears his crest upon a chapeau as does a family of Ledwich, one branch of which bears it as a charge.

Crest coronets may have always *implied* rank but their early heraldic use was as a decoration rather than a firm indication of the armiger's status. Nowadays the ducal crest coronet of three strawberry leaves (not to be confused with a duke's coronet) is never granted and its use permitted only in the case of those arms originating earlier. Its use by a number of Irish families, Norman, Gaelic and Anglo-Irish, has not been uncommon in the past, so descent from an ancient peerage family should not be assumed nor, indeed, should any royal relationship.

A chapeau, also called a cap of dignity or cap of maintenance.

In 1665 Charles II granted royal warrants to the officers of arms of Ireland and Scotland to allow the peers of the two countries to wear the same coronets as those of like rank in England. The assignment of a coronet to a baron dates only from this reign and the codification of types of coronet for different ranks of the peerage from little earlier. Formerly coronets of all types were worn according to the taste of the wearer, who might have been anything from knight to king. The assigned sorts of coronets of rank are: for a duke, a circle of gold with eight strawberry leaves set upon the rim; for a marquis, a circle of gold with four strawberry leaves alternating with as many spikes ensigned with pearls; for an earl, eight spikes ensigned with pearls, alternately on the rim as many strawberry leaves; for a viscount, a gold circle with sixteen pearls on the rim; for a baron, a circle of gold with six pearls. The crown vallery, the pallisado crown, the celestial crown and the mural coronet are not coronets of rank and while no strict rules for their use exist they are not granted easily.

The antique Irish crown is discussed in the context of its occurence in the arms of Ireland. This is not the crown most likely to be observed in personal arms or crests, even of those known to be chiefs of their names. Far more likely to be met is the common enough ducal crest coronet. Whatever form of crown we find in the armory of Ireland, and at whatever date, if meant as an indication of royalty, must have been a quite late borrowing from foreign custom. It is fairly certain that no Irish king, great or small, ever actually wore a crown as a mark of his office.

The National and Provincial Arms

The arms of Ireland are: *Azure, a harp or, stringed argent.*
The national emblem is the harp not the shamrock. The
harp appears on the president's banner, our coinage, our
tax demands. If you appropriate it to your own use you
do so at your peril, for the law forbids use of the harp
or anything resembling the harp. Its thirteenth century
inclusion in the *Armorial Wijnbergen* has already been
referred to, but it is well known that for the period of
England's lordship of Ireland the arms recorded and
borne were, *Azure, three crowns or.* In Ireland these are
now the arms of the province of Munster but this
charge, and sometimes the entire coat, is widely shared
in other heraldic jurisdictions. We find it as the bearing
of the German city of Cologne; of the diocese of Cracow
in Poland; of the city of Colchester in England. It is the
national coat of arms of Sweden and even that attributed
to the preheraldic king Arthur, hero of ancient British
legend. Clearly this antique crown, often called an
antique *Irish* crown, is understood throughout Europe as
a symbol of authority, though not necessarily of kingship.
It can be seen on a thirteenth century crozier head
found near the Rock of Cashel, seat of the kings of
Munster. Its application in this way implies both temporal
and spiritual power. Triplicated to fit the shape of a
shield it becomes an heraldic coat. When Robert de
Vere, favourite of Richard II, was created Lord of Ireland
in 1386 he was granted the privilege of quartering these

The arms of Ireland, first recorded about 1275. The crest dates from the time of Richard II and probably originates from one of his personal badges.

arms with his own. Presumably this ceased with his fall from grace, but *Azure, three crowns or* remained Ireland's national arms until the time of Henry VIII. He, perhaps to lend an air of legitimacy to his assumption of the title "King of Ireland", perhaps to avoid any similarity to the three crowns of the Papal arms, adopted the more ancient harp. It was remarked at the time that the reason for the choice of the harp as the emblem of Ireland was that the country and the instrument were as troublesome to tune, and each as little worth the effort!

The crest of Ireland, a deer springing from a tower, probably originated in the borrowing of a white hart from a badge of Richard II. He was, after all, one of the few English monarchs to take the trouble to visit Ireland in an effort to order her affairs. He did appoint the first Ireland King of Arms. It is possible that his interest in Irish heraldic matters extended to allowing or encouraging the use of one of his own heraldic devices as part of the national arms. This crest has always appeared upon a wreath, unlike those of England and Scotland that appear upon crowns—an indication that at its time of origin Ireland's constitutional status was still that of lordship rather than kingdom, and separate from the kingdom of England.

Though known worldwide as a an emblem of Ireland the shamrock has no official status in Irish heraldry and it began to assume significance only late in the seventeenth century. It does have some protection as a national emblem in that it is no longer likely to be allowed to a private petitioner. Where it is encountered in earlier arms it will probably be found that it is blazoned simply as a trefoil vert. (Though not, for example, in the case of Hackett.) The shamrock certainly appears in English heraldry, as a royal badge of Ireland, at a period when it was being used here as a revolutionary symbol.

It is perhaps the right time to remark that the colour green, although mentioned in a quasi-heraldic context by at least one Gaelic author of the 15th century, is something of a newcomer as a national colour. Inasmuch as there was any colour long associated with Ireland, that colour appears to have been "St Patrick's Blue". Only as late as the middle of the eighteenth century did green begin to acquire a popularity. The field of the national arms has been blue since its earliest recording. The antique crown of the crozier head is set in blue enamel. In Gaelic legend and literature Mór Mumhan who, when wedded to the rightful king of Munster, becomes the sovereignty of Munster incarnate, is usually said to be a beauty robed in deep blue. These associations with Munster are at least as ancient as the known usage of the same emblemology for the arms of the country as a whole.

The harp of Leinster appears to be a borrowing from the national arms. Its use, with the arms of the other ancient kingdoms of Ireland now called provinces, was well known at the middle of the seventeenth century. Their use quartered, though common, has no authority. The first official notice of their quartering together was in 1733 when they were remarked by William Hawkins Ulster. By then of course the Kingdom of Meath, approximating to modern Meath and Westmeath, had ceased to be. Royal Meath, at Tara of the Kings the focus of the High Kingship of Ireland, is represented heraldically by a king upon his throne.

The arms of Ulster are quite clearly composed of the red hand of the O'Neills which has been discussed elsewhere, and the red cross of the de Burghos who became de Burgh and finally Burke. Veterans of the crusades, in all likelihood their cross derives from the

The arms of the four provinces.

crosses of cloth that were stitched to the outer garments of the crusaders in the century before the use of coat-armour was widely established. Walter de Burgh, Lord of Connaught, was created Earl of Ulster in 1243 and the association of the arms and the territory dates from then. Ulster, we should remind ourselves, includes Donegal, Cavan and Monaghan. The arms of the modern province of Northern Ireland have a white field rather than the de Burgh yellow, the red cross is charged, not with an inescutcheon, but a white mullet of six points upon which appears the red hand and above which is a royal crown.

Though it is relatively easy to identify the origin of the arms of Ulster, Munster, Leinster and Meath, those of Connacht provide some opportunity for speculation. These arms, the dimidation of an eagle displayed and an armed hand, bear a close resemblance to the arms of the Schottenkloster (Irish monastery) at Regensburg in Bavaria, and it may well be asked why. We know that certain Irish rulers, including Donnchadh and Domhnall MacCarthy, princes of Desmond, were allowed the use of these arms. They were, presumably, amongst the monastery's benefactors and this concession was a gesture of friendship. The Vatican document that records their deaths and the fact concerning the arms also notes the death, in 1198, of Ruairi O'Connor, King of Connacht. If, like the Desmond royalty, Ruari was conceded the use of such arms of affection then there exists an heraldic link between the eleventh-century German religious house and the modern province of Connacht. The evidence is incomplete but the hypothesis is plausible.

Arms of Noncombatants

Though coat armour was at first the preserve of knights and the holders of feudal territories it had not been long in existence before the dignity of bearing arms was sought by others whose appearance on the battlefield would be inappropriate or impossible. In particular we should mention the bearing of arms by ladies.

A lady may bear, by courtesy, her father's arms if she is unmarried. During her marriage her husband is presumed to bear arms for her though she may, should she choose, bear his. As a widow she may bear the arms of her late husband, impaled with her own if she is an heiress. It was unimaginable in the Middle Ages that a married woman would bear arms in her own right. She was virtually her husband's property and as such could have no property of her own, including arms. Even those she might acquire by inheritance would be borne by her husband during their marriage and by her children, quartered, after her death. It seems that she was regarded as a person of importance when she was a marriage prospect, possibly with her father's property to come to her. As a widow, again with the possibility of her being in control of property, she resumed her armigerous status. These are general rules though we know of a grant to a woman, to bear arms in her own right, before heraldry's first century was over and other, later, grants to married women, but they are exceptions. As a married woman she hardly existed heraldically—an

The arms of Baroness Kieth, displayed upon a losenge rather than a shield. The "gas-bracket" compartment was much in use in the last century when this emblazonment appeared as part of an obituary notice.

oddly unchivalrous attitude in a science intimately bound up with chivalry and born in an age when gentlemen professed to hold women all but sacred!

A lady bears her arms upon a losenge rather than a shield. If she is unmarried it is surmounted by a blue riband tied in a true-lover's knot. Again, it is possible to cite exceptions, for we know of grants to women of arms to be borne upon a shield. Quite how a lady with her own right to arms should bear those arms seems never to have been strictly codified—further neglect of a lady's interests in the age of chivalry. That an armigerous lady may transmit her arms is certain; otherwise the only certain rules are negative ones. Namely, that her personal use of her father's arms must cease during her marriage, and that no woman excepting a sovereign, let her be maid or matron, may be granted, use, inherit or transmit any helmet, wreath, mantling, crest or motto.

Just as a lady is not a warrior and does not require a helmet, real or heraldic, so it is customary, though by no means a rule, that clergymen do not display a helmet even though they may have inherited the right to do so. A priest of the Reformed Church when granted arms may have a crest for the use of his heirs noted in the margin of his grant. Should he become a bishop or archbishop he would be allowed a mitre to be borne above the shield and may impale the arms of his see with his personal coat. In an attempt to demilitarise the appearance of the arms of clerics they have sometimes been emblazoned on a cartouche which, though strictly a type of shield, has not the implications of the more usual shape. Priests of the Roman Catholic Church, like their Protestant counterparts, do not display a helmet and crest, for which Church dignitaries substitute a tasselled hat. The hereditary transmission of all or any

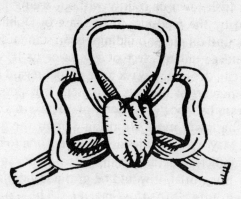

A true-lover's knot which surmounts the arms of an unmarried lady.

part of such an achievement does not arise, though again we may encounter archiepiscopal arms impaled with the personal coat. The impaled coat of the present Archbishop of Dublin, Dr Desmond Connell, presents an interesting juxtaposition of Christian and earlier symbolism.

The use of personal arms as the arms of a feudal territory has been examined earlier. Following the separation of blood and fief, and the eventual passing of feudalism, it became necessary to establish arms that stood for the territory and its community, which in these times is represented by its corporation or council. The means of acquisition of such arms has also been mentioned. The borrowing of portions of the feudal lord's achievement or that of another important family has been seen in the arms of Ulster. Others make use of charges that typify the area or commemorate some event in its history. The grim arms of Derry are amongst the most memorable. Other examples of such corporate arms are easy to find in Ireland. It is hardly possible to enter an Irish town or county without seeing its arms displayed by the roadside. In the case of Dublin they may be found on public buildings, lamp standards, litter bins or indeed on any piece of city property. It is a pity that the city does not always have proper regard for the correct tinctures of its coat. At present it is possible to see at least two bogus versions of these arms in use around the town: most surprisingly upon the gates of the Lord Mayor's official residence. (Were one to remind the city fathers that if heraldry is to mean anything accuracy is essential, it would be in the hope that they might enquire into this matter.) The complete achievement includes a fur cap which is found as part of only two others: those of London and Norwich. This is the headgear of an official, for a corporate entity is incapable of wearing this or any other hat. They are therefore not granted helmets.

As both physical and spiritual communities express their corporate identity by their arms, so other bodies bear arms to express a community of interest. In this category might be included the arms of the ancient Dublin guilds; of schools and colleges; of hospitals and other worthy institutions. An interesting survival is the achievement of arms displayed by the Painter's Union in Dublin, by virtue of its claim of descent from the Guild of St Luke the Evangelist. Though no supporting documentary evidence for that claim exists and the arms in question are derelict, a case for the use of at least similar arms can certainly be made, for the two bodies represent the same community of interest. The guild was composed of painters, paperstainers and cutlers. The emblazonment at present on the union's premises in Aungier Street is far from the best possible, but licensed herald painters were not always members of that guild and sometimes in dispute with it.

Differencing and Distinction

Always allowing that in heraldry, and in Gaelic heraldry most markedly, there is a desire to make dynastic allusions, its original and continuing purpose is to identify individuals. So, when one speaks of the arms of a family one means the arms of the head of the family, the pronominal coat. How then, through his arms, is your son to be told apart from you? And what of your second son, your third son, and so on to the limit of your poor wife's durability? Bear in mind that your cousins (to various degrees, depending upon the point of origin of the arms in the family's history) also have some share in this piece of family property. The use of the same coat by all must result in confusion and the negation of the *raison d'être* of heraldry. It is therefore necessary to difference the arms in some way, either by a change of tincture or the addition or exclusion of charges.

Differencing by changing the tincture of either the field or the charges was common in early days but is also used to differentiate between families bearing similar arms but of no known blood relationship, even though in some cases they share a surname. Similar coats of the same tinctures however, with more or fewer charges, are likely to indicate kinship. For an Irish example we may look at arms of various branches of the great tribe of O'Neill. As we have seen, the earliest known coat for this family (fourteenth century) has a single charge, the

The seal of Owen Roe O'Neill. (Seventeenth century)

dexter hand apaumée. The seal of Owen Roe O'Neill (seventeenth century) has the hand supported by two lions, in chief there are three mullets of six points, in base a salmon naient. Other variations used by different members of the family at various times have only the hand and the salmon, though swimming through water rather than apparently floating in space; as the last example though with the lions; as Owen Roe's but with estoilles rather than mullets and the salmon in water; with normal (five pointed) mullets on a chief of a different tincture, salmon but no water; with hand, lions and salmon but no mullets or estoilles. All of these are clearly variations of the same coat, at once identifying individuals and identifying them *with* their famous family. There is no indication of any systemised differencing to denote degrees of cadency in this example. Presumably whatever seemed appropriate was adopted.

Other early methods of differencing, between families and (more often) within the same family, were the

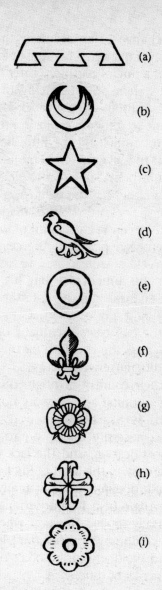

Marks of cadency, used to difference the arms of first to ninth sons. (a) Label, (b) Crescent, (c) Mullet, (d) Martlet, (e) Annulet, (f) Fleur-de-lis, (g) Rose, (h) Cross moline, (i) octofoil.

addition or change of an ordinary; the addition of a label, a canton, a quarter, a bordure or an inescutcheon; the change of a line of partition. Later there evolved in England the system of differencing the coats of nine sons by the addition of the label for the first son, crescent for the second son, mullet for the third, martlet for the fourth, annulet for the fifth, fleur-de-lis for the sixth, rose for the seventh, cross moline for the eighth and for the ninth a double quatrefoil. Should there be further sons a father has the right to assign what marks of difference he pleases. These marks are properly positioned at the centre chief point of the shield though they are often seen placed at the centre point of an ordinary. An eldest son ceases to use his mark of difference on his inheritance but his brothers retain theirs for life and transmit them, further differenced, to their sons. Should any of them at any time marry an heiress and the two coats eventually be absorbed into one by quartering, the necessity for the continuing use of marks of difference would cease.

Even in their country of origin the application of these rules is optional and they are not always strictly kept, though, as has been observed, differencing of some sort is a necessity if arms are to be a functional means of identification, and the lack of it is, at very least, a discourtesy to the head of the house. The use of this formal code of differencing, naturally enough, found its way into Anglo-Irish heraldry though it was by no means universally applied. However, when confirmations of arms were commonly sought from Ulster King's office it was usual to avoid any confusion or risk of offence by adding two marks of difference.

Sometimes a blazon will state that this or that charge is "for distinction" rather than "for difference." The distinction between that armiger and those that lack such a change to the same basic coat is either to make abundantly clear that no blood relationship exists or, more usually, as a mark of bastardy. It must be said at once that such an indication of illegitimacy is not meant as a mark of disgrace to the armiger but should be regarded as a mark of cadency indicating that he cannot inherit his father's property. In earlier times there was no stigma attached to illegitimacy and such children were generally acknowledged as belonging to the family and cherished equally with their half-brothers and half-sisters. But it would surely have been a matter of some importance to those likely to inherit that there should be no uncertainty about which was the legitimate line. Until late in the eighteenth century there was no established rule as to how bastardy should be indicated heraldically. Thereafter the bordure-wavy was adopted for the purpose in England and Ireland. Formerly various devices had been employed, amongst them a border, a label and, best known though perhaps least used, a bend sinister. The common reference to a "bar sinister" for this purpose is not only incorrect, it is ridiculous. A very little thought will reveal that a bar can be neither sinister nor dexter. It is generally agreed that this mistake was born of the confusion between "bar" and the French "barre" meaning "bend."

Bend, bendlet, baton, barre, bar or bordure: all have become, in that context, merely matters for historical discussion as far as the heraldry of most of Ireland is concerned, for in these more charitable times there no longer exists in the law of the Republic any such thing as illegitimacy.

The Marshalling of Arms

The marshalling of arms concerns the conjoining of two or more coats to form a single shield of arms. We know that the addition of differences to arms within a family has sometimes been a matter of choice, imposed on the shield or not according to the bearer's feeling for heraldic nicety, and with no reference to any authority. The marshalling of arms however, while not compulsory, if affected at all by the armiger is the business of the herald.

Arms may be marshalled by dimidation, which is simply the division per pale of two coats, the dexter of one being joined to the sinister of the other, as in the arms of Connacht for example. In the case of the arms of two families being joined to denote a marriage, or in earlier days the joining of two properties by marriage, the arms of the husband appear on the dexter side and those of the wife on the sinister. A Norman-Irish example is the dimidation of the coats of Clare (Or, three chevrons gules) and Fitzgerald (Argent, a saltire gules) which coat was eventually to appear on the seal of the Provosts of Youghal. The result is often confusing visually and the effect may vary from comical to ugly. In the case of two simple coats, each charged with the same honourable ordinary, it is difficult to recognise that two coats are represented at all, the appearance being of a species, of counterchanging. Where figures are involved the effect is yet more odd, for example three lions with the sterns of boats for hind quarters is well known.

This inelegant means of marshalling did not remain long in favour. Impalement, that is the display of two complete coats side by side within the one shield, was found more effective and pleasing. It is difficult within this format to retain the classic triangulism of the shield, but it is more nearly approached than through dimidation. A remnant of the practice of dimidation is seen in the method of impaling a bordured shield: the bordure is curtailed at the pale.

It is likely that the quartering of arms preceded both of these methods of marshalling and remains in use to the present. A basic quartering places the male coat in the first and fourth quarters and the female in the second and third. This is not the coat of a married man, rather that of his children. During his wife's life and after the death of her father, should he wish the two coats marshalled together they might be conjoined by impalement, as would the arms of a widow assuming the responsibility of her late spouse's property. Alternatively he may place the arms of his heiress wife's family, from which he derives a part of his property, upon a small shield within his own, called an "escutcheon of pretence." After his death his children would quarter these arms.

The rules and opinions on the propriety of quartering a previously quartered coat—who is entitled to bear what—are beyond the scope of this work. Enough to say that we encounter multiple quarterings including the heraldically correct but arithmetically inventive "quarterly of six', or even more. The continental fondness for being able to claim sixteen or even thirty-two quarters is not common here, nor, we may be pleased, the style of heraldry it produces. In the course of a family marrying numerous heiresses over generations, a shield

Two coats conjoined by impalement.

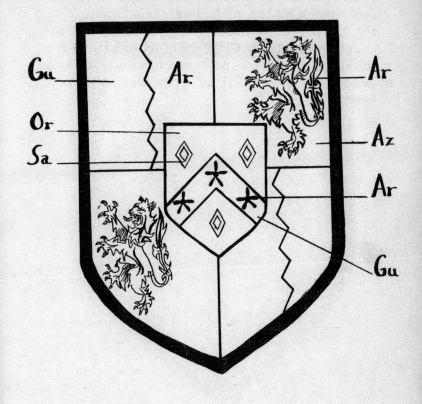

The quartered coat of Rice with the addition of an inescutcheon for Spring. This emblazonment includes an example of tricking to indicate colours.

so cluttered as to be all but unreadable can be produced. Sometimes it is necessary for this to be refined to leave the arms of only the most important families involved.

A characteristically Gaelic use of the division of the shield into quarters does not necessarily denote dynastic alliances and is discussed more appropriately in terms of heraldic design.

Heraldic Art and Design

The heraldic artist has considerable latitude in his representation of a blazon. For example, a shield may be any shape that is recognisable as a shield. While gules must be red, the shade of red is any which pleases the artist or his client. Between them they may decide on anything from vermilion to carmine. The same is true of vert, azure and the rest. An "eagle displayed sable" must be black and it must be displayed, that is, it must have its wings fully spread; but the taste of the artist dictates whether it will be a fat or thin eagle, a fearsome eagle or a jolly one. Equally, though the position of the helmet and the tinctures of the mantling must correspond to certain rules, the helmet may be in the style of any period while the mantling may be a naturalistic drawing, the most rudimentary stylisation, or a vast confection resembling a bed of seaweed which completely surrounds the entire achievement. Supporters may stand on a compartment resembling a hillock or precariously balanced on one looking like a piece of wrought iron; sometimes they float in thin air. All these styles of armorial art have had their periods of popularity. For these reasons the same coat of arms by two different herald painters may not always appear the same to the unpractised eye. It must be kept in mind that the heraldic details do not change despite changes of taste in how they shall be represented. There are to be found in Ireland emblazonments of arms by country craftsmen that are difficult enough to interpret. The injunction issued to unlicenced herald painters of the seventeenth century not only allowed Ulster King to collect due fees for heraldic services but ensured that coats were properly recorded.

The further in time from the battlefield or the tourney that armory was employed, the further the knowledge of heraldic painters decreased in proportion. For example, the jousting shield with its convenient slot for supporting a lance at the dexter chief was realistically represented when it was actually used. Later artists apparently thought that a shield would look altogether better with some visual balancing and deprived it of a similar piece at the sinister. After that heraldic shields assumed such curves and scrolls that they are only recognised for what they are by the presence of charges. The scroll upon which appears the motto also allowed the artist some opportunity for the exercise of his own taste.

The florid fashion of the eighteenth century or the very realistic beasts of the early nineteenth may indicate when a particular emblazonment was painted, but for clues to the actual age and origin of the coat itself one must look deeper. Indications are to be found in the charges used and their disposition upon the field. The arms of certain Norman families are simple and demonstrate the type of heraldic composition originating with the purely practical considerations of shield design and ready recognisablity. The ordinaries which were probably a part of the shield's structure; the single large charge that fills the shield; the triplicated charge that fits its basically triangular shape: these are the marks of a shield of the period of true military heraldry or a design in that tradition.

Gaelic heraldry, on the other hand, being non-military, had no reason to observe and continue the traditions of design founded on a real shield's function. In early examples ordinaries are unknown. For the sake of including as much information as the first user thought important, symmetry with the shield shape is often ignored, as in McDonnell and O'Friel. The placement upon such shields of several different charges which lack visual relationship to each other or the shield's outline indicate that their symbolism created sufficient impact to make graphic considerations of secondary importance. The medium had small relevance to the intended message. That is not to say that graphic devices were never recognised and employed. For example quartering, as used in the arms of O'Hagan, McGrath and others, does not record alliances but is a borrowing from Norman and English practice. Its very incongruity with the shield shape helps to display to better advantage the symbols of the armiger's choice. (In the case of O'Hagan we see a further borrowing in the use of the canton.)

Another factor in the making of military heraldic art is dismissed in that the field of a Gaelic shield is not unusually green, as in the arms of O'Reilly. In this coat as in that of O'Kelly, O'Neill, Egan, O'Fogarty, and numerous others, we find the use of supporters in a characteristically Gaelic way: inside the shield supporting the central charge rather than outside bearing up the shield itself. A recurring mode of design, which despite its symmetrical and English appearance is found in enough Gaelic shields for it to be recognised as popular with the native Irish, places the principal charge in the centre of the shield with a minor charge triplicated around it, as in the arms of O'Molloy, O'Dwyer, O'Malone and MacGorman. At least as common is a principal charge with the secondary charge duplicated at the dexter and sinister points of the chief, as in the arms of

The arms of O'Hagan. Perhaps better thought of as *party per cross* to display each of the charges more prominently. It is not quartered to denote marriages.

The arms of O'Kelly, supporters within the shield in the
Gaelic manner. The crest, an enfield, is peculiar to this sept.

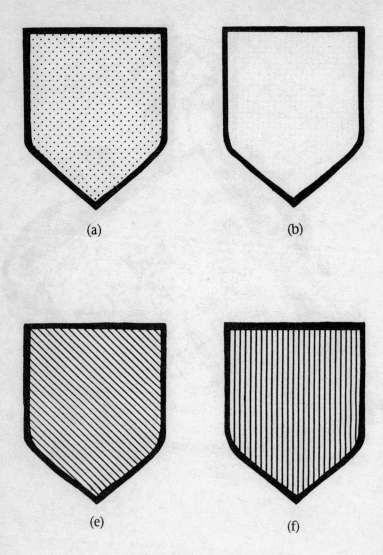

(a) (b)

(e) (f)

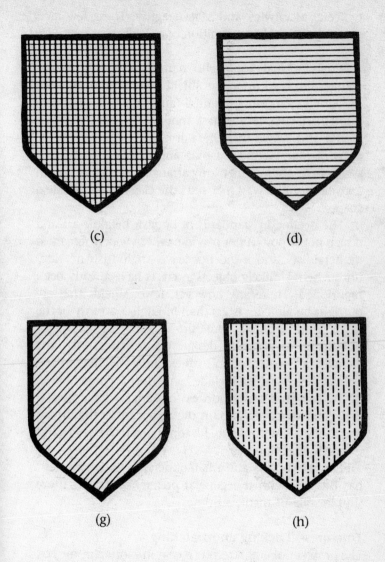

Standardised hatching to represent tinctures: (a) Or, (b) Argent, (c) Sable, (d) Azure, (e) Vert, (f) Gules, (g) Purpure, (h) Orange.

O'Keefe, MacAwley and MacGeraghty. These few facts remembered make recognition of a Gaelic coat relatively easy.

Coats related to Gaelic names exhibiting Gaelic charges disposed upon the shield according to the taste of Dublin's English-appointed (and sometimes English-trained) heralds represent a transitional stage between Gaelic and Anglo-Irish heraldry. For example, in the arms of Mac Sweeney, Doyle and O'Byrne, our Celtic symbols persist but are trimly arranged around or within an ordinary in a way that suits the classic Gothic shield shape.

The decline in standards of English heraldic art and design in the post-Tudor period has been widely remarked by heraldists, and it did not leave Anglo-Irish heraldry untouched. Unlikely objects as crests have already been mentioned. There are, however, fewer shields that are outright heraldic disasters than in English armory of the same period, though some are certainly overcrowded. The nadir of armorial design was reached with the "landscape" coats. For an Irish example we may cite the arms of Gough which include "on a chief a representation of the east wall of the fortress of Tarifa, with a breach between two turrets and on the dexter turret the British flag flying". The complete blazon is given elsewhere and is worth attention.

The last century and a half of heraldic enlightenment has brought with it a general preference for the more simple style of medieval times.

Tinctures—Tricking and Hatching
The problem of emblazoning a coat in monochrome has been solved in two ways: by tricking and by hatching. If one wishes to make a note of an achievement an outline sketch can be made and the field, charges and

accessories marked with the standard abbreviations for the tinctures. They are: Or, Gold; A (sometimes Ar), Silver; Sa, Black; Gu, Red; Az, Blue; Vt, Green; Purp, Purple; Pr, Proper; Ten, Tenné; San, Sanguine/Murrey. The two last are rare and even more so are the orange-tawny, and certain tertiary colours mentioned by the heraldic writers of the past. When a charge occurs more than once it may be drawn once and the figures 2, 3, etc. placed at the relevant positions.

While tricking is a useful herald's shorthand it will clearly not do for stonecarving, woodcarving, metal casting or engraving. A system of hatching has long been understood as being standard. It is likely to be encountered in examples of work produced up to the the end of the last century but is seldom used nowadays. Official records have always been either coloured or tricked.

Gallimaufry

Heraldry has been aptly enough called "the shorthand of history", but it is more: it is a short-cut through the study of history. Were one to take any shield of arms seen on or in an Irish building and ask, "To whom was it granted and when?", the answer would open a dozen roads into at least a century of political and social history. Heraldry fires and fuels the curiosity like few other studies. The questions it prompts are for the most part answerable. Those that are not are the basis of speculation ranging from learned to lunatic. Lack of complete knowledge has not deterred all manner of people from setting themselves up as authorities. And the last hundred and fifty years has not lacked scholars ready to separate the unsound and downright bogus assertions of others from opinions founded on facts, sometimes with a savagery that does not become academics. Into the present century it seems to have been difficult to offer an opinion about any heraldic matter without having another heraldist, well, up in arms. The study of the *study* of heraldry is yet another by-road offered.

Heraldic specimen hunting is an engaging occupation which, once surrendered to, leads one through Dublin's cathedrals to view the arms of the sees, the stall plates of the Knights of St Patrick and of Irishmen who distinguished themselves here and abroad; along Galway's high street to see examples of impaled arms in that

The impaled coat of Archbishop Murray, associated with the Sisters of Charity at the time of the Order's foundation. This example of heraldic specimen hunting was drawn with the aid of binoculars from the emblazonment at 56, St Stephen's Green, previously St Vincent's Hospital.

city's marriage stones and ask "Were these families amongst the Tribes of Galway? Were they native or Norman?"; in our gumboots across fields to many a ruined abbey to examine the memorial to the one who endowed it and those who displaced him. There continues a sense of discovery with every coat recognised. There increases an understanding of one man's reasons for living or dying at this place and at that time. It is natural enough to wonder what became of his descendants.

At Kilfane in County Kilkenny we may see the longest surviving piece of armorial stone carving in Ireland: an effigy of the knight Geoffery de Cantwell whose name also survives. The Royal Hospital chapel at Kilmainham has examples of heraldic stained glass windows so valued that during the Emergency they were plucked from the walls and buried. At Marsh's library repose some of the country's best examples of heraldic bookplates. In Christ Church is what we call Strongbow's tomb but which does not display the arms of de Clare; in its crypt is a memorial to one Natahaniel Sneyd whose coat (Argent a scythe, blade in chief handle in bend sinister, on the fess point a fleur-de-lis all sable) provides a slightly obscure example of *armes parlantes*, for is the handle of a scythe not called a sned and does it not remind us of the German verb, schneiden, "to cut"? And more, we learn that the fleur-de-lis commemorates these arms being honourably borne at the battle of Poictiers in 1356. Above St Stephen's Green is an ecclesiastical coat that is challenging enough to identify by the glimpse provided from the top deck of a Dublin bus. Nearby, in the porch of the University Church, are displayed the arms of its founder and founder of the Catholic University, John Cardinal Newman.

This is a mere handful of examples of Irish armory that may be encountered before setting foot in a museum. Indeed before passing through the door of the National Museum of Ireland we see a huge relief emblazonment of the arms of the Baker's Guild. Inside we are offered the opportunity to view the fourteenth century Book Shrine of Domhnach Airgid, the makers of which were so devoted to their faith and to heraldry that they decorated it with arms they attributed to the Saviour himself. In a nearby room we may see exhibited the heraldic regalia of the continental orders with which past Presidents of Ireland were invested. On the same street, at the Chief Herald's Office, is the National Heraldic Museum, the only one of its kind in the world, where is to be seen a herald's regalia of earlier times and that of a Knight of St Patrick, heraldic banners of Chiefs of Irish names, the colours of the Irish regiments that served the crown of France, armorial pottery and glass, seals of individuals and institutions, grants of arms, heraldically engraved gemstones. Enough variety of armorial display to satisfy any heraldry enthusiast? Perhaps so, but it is barely ten per cent of the precious material that might be shown did space allow.

Delightful as may be such a national collection of heraldic treasures, its operation is only incidental to the true work of heralds and genealogical research advisers which goes on in the same building. A herald's opinion has, if not the force of law, then authority enough to frame the terms of legal documents upon which judicial opinion may at some time be based. A precedent set by a herald in an action on behalf of the state is a matter of public record and likely to be acted upon by his successsors. They are therefore properly cautious and would usually rather act upon a precedent than create one. In Ireland the Chief Herald works within the

Department of the Taoiseach.

In a chapter of diverse heraldic facts it may be mentioned that a notable heraldic precedent was set by Ireland in a grant of arms to the late President John F. Kennedy, the only known instance of a state conferring a grant upon the head of another sovereign state. The blazon, reminiscent of ancient arms of both Kennedy and Fitzgerald, its American element in the crest, is given elsewhere. More recently the Office of the Chief Herald has been responsible for contributing to the internationalism of heraldry by its origination of the design for the flag of the European Community. Irish heraldry, with its roots in the medieval ideal of unified Europe, has assisted the ancient aspiration toward becoming a political fact.

The continuation of the traditions of heraldry by this office, and other heraldic authorities worldwide with which it co-operates, is not merely the work of civil servants nor that of dry as dust academic historians. It is the means whereby the Middle Ages and the yet deeper past reach out and touch our own time.

A Short Irish Armory

The manuscripts of the Genealogical Office are the main source of Irish heraldic information. From these Sir Bernard Burke Ulster made the Irish entries in the *General Armory* and Patrick Kennedy, Herald Painter at the Office of Arms, made his collection of "Sketches". From records at the same office was compiled Roger O'Feral's "Linea Antiqua" which was the basis of Edward MacLysaght's widely circulated list of blazons of arms of the principal Gaelic and Norman families. The following list, though drawn from several previous compilations and personal notes, has the same ultimate source. The most common Irish names associated with the bearing of arms are listed, with the addition of several other names mentioned elsewhere in this book. It is only intended as a pocket reference as it would be possible to duplicate, indeed multiply, most of the names here citing numerous grants and confirmations and, of course, different blazons. Those seeking further information should refer to Burke's *General Armory* which, despite any shortcomings claimed for it, is the most extensive available work.

Aherne: Vert, three herons argent. Crest: a pelican in her piety proper.

MacAuliffe: Argent, three mermaids with combs and mirrors in fess azure between as many mullets of the last. Crest: A boar's head couped or.

MacAwley: Argent a lion rampant gules armed and langued azure in chief two dexter hands couped at the wrist of the second. Crest: A demi-lion rampant gules.

Barrett: Barry of ten per pale argent and gules counterchanged. Crest: A demi-lion rampant sable ducally crowned per pale argent and gules.

Barry: Argent three bars gemels gules.

O'Beirne: Argent an orange tree eradicated and fructed proper, in base a lizard vert, in the dexter base point a saltire couped gules, on a chief azure the sun in his splendour or and a crescent of the first. Crest: A dexter arm in armour embowed the hand grasping a sword all proper.

Blake: Argent a fret gules. Crest: A leopard passant proper.

O'Boland: Argent a lion passant gules langued and armed azure, on a chief or an eagle displayed of the third. Crest: A demi-lion rampant argent.

O'Boyle: Or an oak tree eradicated vert. Crest: A sword point upwards proper and a passion cross or in saltire surmounted of a heart gules.

O'Boylan: Argent an eagle displayed sable armed or.

MacBrady: Sable, in the sinister base a dexter hand couped at the wrist proper pointing with index finger to the sun in his splendour in dexter chief or.

O'Brennan (Ossory): Gules two lions rampant combatant supporting a garb or, in chief three swords two in saltire points upwards and one in fess point to the dexter, pommels and hilts of the second. Crest: An arm embowed in armour grasping a sword all proper.

O'Brennan (Connacht): Argent a lion rampant azure, in chief two dexter hands couped at the wrist apaumée gules. Crest: Out of a ducal coronet or a plume of five ostrich feathers alternately azure and or.

O'Brien (Ancient): Gules, a dexter arm issuant from the sinister flank the hand proper grasping a sword in pale.

O'Brien (Modern): Gules three lions passant guardant in pale per pale or and argent.

Brooke: Or a cross engrailed per pale gules and sable. Crest: A badger proper.

O'Broder: Per pale gules and sable, on a fess between three griffins" heads erased or as many losenges ermines. Crest: A demi-greyhound sable holding in the paws a dart gules feathered argent.

Browne: Or an eagle with two heads displayed sable.

de Burgh (Earl of Ulster, Lord of Connacht): Or a cross gules.

Burke (Earl of Clanricarde, Chief of his House): Or a cross gules, in the dexter canton a lion rampant sable. Crest: A cat-a-mountain sejant guardant proper collared and chained or.

MacWilliam Burke: Or a cross gules, in the dexter canton a lion rampant sable, in the sinister a sinister hand apaumée argent.

Butler: Quarterly: 1st and 4th, Or a chief indented azure; 2nd and 3rd, Gules, three covered cups or. Crest: Out of a ducal coronet or a plume of five ostrich feathers argent, therefrom issuant a falcon rising of the last.

O'Byrne: Gules a chevron between three dexter hands apaumée couped at the wrist argent.

MacCabe: Vert a fess wavy between three salmon naiant argent. Crest: A demi-griffon segreant.

O'Cahill (Munster): Argent a whale spouting in the sea proper. Crest: An anchor erect cable twined around the stock all proper.

O'Callaghan: Argent in base a mount vert on the dexter side a hurst of oak trees issuant therefrom a wolf passant towards the sinister all proper.

MacCann: Azure fretty or, on a fess argent a boar passant gules. Crest: a salmon naiant proper.

O'Carroll: Sable two lions rampant combatant or armed and langued gules supporting a sword point upwards proper pommel and hilt of the first.

MacCartan: Vert a lion rampant or, on a chief argent a crescent between two dexter hands couped at the wrist gules. Crest: A lance erect or headed argent entwined with a snake descending vert.

MacCarthy: Argent a stag trippant gules attired and unguled or.

O'Casey: Argent a chevron between three eagles' heads erased gules.

O'Cassidy: Per chevron argent and gules, in chief two lions rampant and in base a boar passant both counterchanged. Crest: A spear broken in three pieces two in saltire and the head in pale proper banded gules.

Cavendish (Baron Waterpark): Sable three bucks' heads caboshed argent. Crest: On a ducal coronet or a snake nowed proper.

MacClancy: Argent two lions passant guardant in pale gules. Crest: A dexter hand couped at the wrist erect holding a sword in pale pierced through a boar's head couped all proper.

O'Clery: Or three nettle leaves vert.

MacCoghlan: Argent three lions passant guardant gules crowned or.

MacColgan: Azure a lion rampant or between three pheons points down argent.

Condon: Argent a lion rampant gules langued and armed azure.

O'Coffey: Vert a fess ermine between three Irish cups or. Crest: A man riding on a dolphin proper.

O'Concannon: Argent on a mount in base proper an oak tree vert, perched on the top thereof a falcon proper, two crosses crosslet fitchée in fess azure. Crest: An elephant sable tusked or.

O'Connell: Per fess argent and vert a stag trippant proper between three trefoils slipped counterchanged.

O'Conor Don: Argent an oak tree vert. Crest: An arm

embowed in armour holding a short sword entwined with a serpent all proper.

O'Connor (of Corcomroe): Vert a stag trippant argent. Crest: A hand in a gauntlet erect holding a broken dart all proper.

O'Conor (Faly): Argent on a mount in base vert an oak tree acorned proper.

O'Connor (Kerry): Vert a lion rampant double queued and crowned or. Crest: A dexter arm embowed in mail proper garnished or the hand grasping a sword erect proper.

O'Connor (Sligo): Per pale vert and argent, in the dexter a lion rampant to the sinister or, in the sinister on a mount in base vert an oak tree proper. Crest: An arm in armour embowed holding a sword all proper.

O'Connolly (Kildare): Argent on a saltire sable five escallops of the field.

O'Conry (Offaly): Quarterly: 1st, Vert three goats passant argent; 2nd, Argent a lion rampant gules; 3rd, Gules three escallops argent; 4th, Vert a cock statant proper. Crest: A blackamoor's head in profile couped at the shoulders sable and bound round the temples with a ribbon argent.

O'Conroy (O'Mulconry): Azure an ancient book open indexed edged or, a chief embattled of the last. Crest: A dexter arm vested or cuffed ermine grasping a wreath of laurel proper.

MacConsidine: Per pale sable and gules three lions passant guardant in pale per pale or and argent armed azure.

Conyngham(Marquis): Argent a shakefork between three mullets sable. Crest: A unicorn's head erased argent armed and maned or.

O'Corrigan: Or a chevron between two trefoils slipt in chief and in base a lizard passant vert. Crest: Two battle axes in saltire in front of a sword proper point downwards pommel and hilt or.

MacCostello: Or three fusils azure. Crest: A falcon proper belled and jessed or.

MacCotter: Azure three evets in pale proper. Crest: A lion passant reguardant proper.

Creagh: Argent a chevron gules between three laurel branches vert, on a chief azure as many bezants. Crest: A horse's head erased argent caparisoned gules in the headstall of the bridle a laurel branch vert.

O'Crean: Argent a wolf rampant sable between three human hearts gules. Crest: A demi-wolf rampant sable holding between the paws a human heart or.

O'Crowley: Argent a boar passant azure between three crosslet gules.

O'Cullane (Collins): Argent two lions rampant combatant proper. Crest a pelican vulning herself wings elevated proper.

O'Cullen: Gules on a chevron between three dexter hands erect couped at the wrist argent a garb of the first between two trefoils slipped vert. Crest: A mermaid with comb and mirror all proper.

O'Cullinan: Argent a stag springing gules attired and unguled vert, in base a dexter hand apaumée couped at the wrist proper.

MacCurtin: Vert in front of a lance in pale or a stag trippant argent attired or between three crosses crosslet or, two and one, and as many trefoils slipped argent one and two. Crest: In front of two lances in saltire argent headed or an Irish harp sable.

Cusack: Per pale or and azure, a fess counterchanged.

D'Alton: Azure a lion rampant guardant argent charged on the shoulder with a crescent sable between five fleurs-de-lis or.

O'Daly: Per fess argent and or a lion rampant per fess

sable and gules, in chief two dexter hands couped at the wrist of the last.

D'Arcy: Azure semée of crosses crosslet and three cinquefoils argent. Crest: On a chapeau gules turned up ermine a bull sable armed or.

O'Davoren: Argent a sword erect in pale distilling drops of blood proper pommelled and hilted or. Crest: A hind statant proper.

O'Dea: Argent a dexter hand fesswise couped at the wrist cuffed indented azure holding a sword in pale all proper, in chief two snakes embowed vert.

O'Dempsey: Gules a lion rampant argent, armed and langued azure between two sword points upwards of the second pommelled and hilted or the dexter bendwise and the other in bend sinister.

MacDermot: Argent on a chevron gules between three boars" heads erased azure tusked and bristled or as many crosses crosslet of the last. Crest: A demi-lion rampant azure holding in the dexter paw a sceptre crowned or.

Dillon: Argent a lion passant between three crescents gules. Crest: A demi-lion rampant gules holding in the paws an estoile wavy or.

O'Dinneen: Azure two swords in saltire points upward argent pommelled and hilted or between four roses of the last. Crest: A stag's head proper.

O'Doherty: Argent a stag springing gules, on a chief vert three mullets of the field.

MacDonagh (Connacht): Per chevron invected or and vert, in chief two lions passant guardant gules in base a boar passant argent armed and crined of the first langued gules. Crest: A dexter arm erect couped at the elbow vested azure cuffed argent holding in the hand a sword erect entwined with a lizard all proper.

MacDonlevy: Argent on a mount in base proper a lion gules and a buck of the second rampant combatant supporting a dexter hand couped at the wrist of the third. Crest: A lion rampant gules.

MacDonnell (Clare and Connaught): Azure an ancient galley sails set and flags flying argent between in chief a cross calvary in three grieces or, between in the dexter an increscent of the second and in the sinister a dexter handcouped at the wrist apaumée proper and in base a salmon naiant of the second. Crest: A unicorn passant gules.

MacDonnell (of the Glens): Quarterly: 1st, Or a lion rampant gules; 2nd, Or a dexter arm issuant from the sinister fess point out of a cloud proper in the hand a cross crosslet fitchée erect azure; 3rd, Argent a lymphad sails furled sable; 4th, Per fess azure and vert a dolphin naiant proper. Crest: A dexter arm embowed fesswise couped at the shoulder vested or cuffed argent holding in the hand proper a cross crossslet fitchée erect azure.

O'Donnell: Or issuing from the sinister side of the shield an arm fesswise vested azure cuffed argent holding in the hand proper a passion cross gules.

O'Donnellan: Argent an oak tree eradicated proper, on the sinister side a slave sable chained to the stem gules. Crest: On a mount proper a lion rampant or.

O'Donnelly: Argent two lions rampant combatant supporting a dexter hand couped apaumée gules, in base the sea therein a salmon naiant proper.

O'Donoghue: Vert two foxes rampant combatant argent, on a chief of the last an eagle volant sable. Crest: A dexter arm in armour embowed holding a sword the blade entwined with a serpent all proper.

O'Donovan: Argent issuing from the sinister side of the shield a cubit dexter arm vested gules cuffed of the first the hand grasping a scian in pale the blade entwined with a serpent all proper. Crest: A falcon alighting or.

O'Dowling: Argent a holly tree eradicated proper, on a

chief azure a lion passant between two trefoils slipped or. Crest: A lion's head erased azure collared gemmelles or.

O'Doran: Per pale sable and argent a boar passant counterchanged, on a chief azure three mullets of the second.

O'Dowd: Vert a saltire or, in chief two swords in saltire points upward the dexter surmounted of the sinister argent pommelled and hilted or.

Doyle: Argent three bucks' heads erased gules attired or, in a border compony counter compony or and azure. Crest: A buck's head couped gules attired argent ducally gorged or.

O'Driscoll: Argent an ancient galley sails furled sable. Crest: A cormorant proper.

O'Duggan: Azure a decrescent argent between nine estoiles of eight points or. Crest: A demi-lion rampant or langued and armed gules.

O'Dunn: Azure an eagle displayed or. Crest: In front of a holly bush proper a lizard passant or.

O'Dwyer: Argent a lion rampant gules between three ermine spots. Crest: A hand couped at the wrist and erect grasping a sword all proper.

MacEgan: Quarterly: 1st, Gules a tower argent supported on either side by two men in full armour each holding in the interior hand a battle-axe all proper, in chief a snake fesswise or; 2nd and 3rd, Or on a bend vert three plates; 4th, as first but the tower ensigned with a swan proper. Crest: Isssuant from the top of a tower argent a demi-man in armour couped at the knees holding in the dexter hand a battle-axe all proper.

MacEvoy: Per fess azure and per pale or and ermine issuant therefrom a demi-lion argent, in the dexter base a dexter hand couped at the wrist of the fourth. Crest: A cubit arm erect vested gules cuffed erminois in the hand a sword proper.

MacEnchroe (Crowe): Argent on a mount vert an oak tree proper, a canton gules carged with an antique Irish crown or. Crest: On a mount vert an Irish wolfhound argent collared gules.

Fagan: Per chevron gules and ermine, in chief three covered cups or. Crest: A griffin argent winged and tufted or supporting in the talons an olive branch vert fructed or.

O'Fahy: Azure a hand couped at the wrist fesswise in chief proper holding a sword palewise argent pommelled and hilted or point downward pierced through a boar's head erased of the last. Crest: A naked arm erect couped below the elbow holding a broken spear all proper point downwards or.

Falkiner: Or three falcons close proper in the centre chief point a mullet gules. Crest: A falcon's lure proper charged with a mullet gules between two wings azure.

O'Fallon: Gules a greyhound rampant argent supporting between the forepaws a tilting spear point to the dexter or. Crest: A demi-greyhound salient argent.

O'Farrell: Vert a lion rampant or. Crest: On a ducal coronet or a greyhound springing sable.

O'Finnegan: Gules two lions rampant combatant supporting a sword in pale blade wavy point upwards proper. Crest: A falcon rising proper.

Fitzgerald (Duke of Leinster): Argent a saltire gules. Crest: An ape proper collared and chained or.

Fitzgerald (Earl of Desmond): Ermine a saltire gules. Crest: A boar passant gules fretty or.

Fitzgerald (Knight of Kerry): Ermine a saltire gules. Crest: A knight on horseback proper.

Fitzgibbon: Ermine a saltire gules, on a chief argent three annulets of the second. Crest: A boar passant gules charged on the body with three annulets fesswise argent.

Fitzpatrick: Sable a saltire argent, on a chief azure three fleurs-de-lis or. Crest: A dragon reguardant vert surmounted of a lion guardant sable dexter paw resting on the dragon's head.

O'Flaherty: Argent two lions rampant combatant supporting a dexter hand couped at the wrist all gules, in base a boat with eight oars sable.

O'Flanagan: Argent out of a mount vert in base an oak tree proper, bordured of the second. A dexter cubit arm in armour proper garnished or and gules holding a flaming sword azure pommelled and hilted of the second.

Fleming: Vair a chief chequey or and gules.

O'Flynn: Azure a wolf passant argent, in chief three bezants. Crest: A dexter hand erect couped holding a serpent rail embowed head to the sinister all proper.

O'Fogarty: Azure two lions rampant combatant supporting a garb all or, in dexter base a crescent argent, in sinister base a harp of the second stringed of the third.

Fox: Argent a lion rampant, in chief two dexter hands couped at the wrist gules. An arm embowed in armour holding a sword all proper.

French: Ermine a chevron sable. Crest: A dolphin embowed proper.

O'Friel: Gules in dexter fess a garb or, in sinister fess a dexter hand couped at the wrist fesswise proper grasping a cross calvary on three grieces argent, in chief three mullets of the second. Crest: A garb or.

O'Gallagher: Argent a lion rampant sable treading on a serpent in fess proper between three trefoils vert. Crest: A crescent gules out of the horns of a serpent erect proper.

O'Galvin: Gules three salmon haurient argent.

O'Gara: Argent three lions rampant azure, on a chief gules a demi-lion rampant or. Crest: A demi-lion rampant ermine holding between the paws a wreath of oak vert acorned or.

MacGarry: Argent a lion rampant between four trefoils slipped, in chief a lizard passant all vert. Crest: A fox's head couped gules holding in the mouth a serpent proper.

O'Garvey: Ermine two chevronels between three crosses patée gules. Crest: A lion passant guardant gules.

MacGenis: Vert a lion rampant or, on a chief argent a dexter hand erect couped at the wrist gules.

MacGilfoyle: Azure two bars argent. Crest: A demi-lion rampant argent holding between the paws a battle-axe erect gules blade of the first.

MacGillycuddy: Gules a wyvern or. Crest: MacGillycuddy's reeks proper.

MacGeoghan: Argent a lion rampant between three dexter hands couped at the wrist gules. Crest: A grey hound passant or.

MacGeraghty: Argent on a mount vert an oak tree proper, in chief two falcons volant gules.

MacGorman: Azure a lion passant between three swords erect argent. Crest: An arm embowed in armour grasping in the hand a sword, blade wavy, all proper.

O'Gormley: Or three martlets gules, two and one.

Gough (Viscount): Quarterly: 1st and 4th, gules on a mount vert a lion passant guardant or, supporting with the dexter paw the Union flag and over the same, in chief, the words "China, India," in letters of gold; 2nd and 3rd, azure on a fess argent between three boars' heads couped or, a lion passant gules (being his family arms), in the centre chief point, pendent from a riband argent fimbrated azure a representation of the badge of the Spanish Order of Charles III proper and on a chief a representation of the east wall of the fortress Tarifa, with a breach between two turrets, and on the dexter turret the British flag flying also proper. Crests: In the centre, on a wreath, a boar's head couped at the neck or; on the dexter side, on a mural crown argent a lion passant guardant or, holding in the dexter paw two flag-staves in bend sinister proper the one bearing the Union flag of Great Britain and Ireland, surmounting the other, the staff thereof broken, with a triangular banner flowing therefrom, being intended to represent a Chinese flag, having thereon the device of a dragon, in an escroll, above the word "China"; on the sinister side, on a wreath, a dexter arm embowed, in the uniform of the 87th. Regiment, being gules faced vert, the hand grasping the colour of the said regiment displayed and a representation of a French eagle reversed and depressed, the staff broken proper in an escroll above the word "Barrosa". Supporters: On the dexter side a lion regardant or, gorged with an eastern crown gules with chain reflexed over the back gold, the rim of the crown inscribed "Punjab" in letters also gold; on the sinister side a dragon (intended to represent the device upon a Chinese flag, granted to Viscount Gough in the crest of honourable augmentation) or, gorged with a mural crown sable inscribed with the word "China", and chained gold.

MacGovern: Azure a lion passant or, in chief three crescents of the last.

O'Grady: Per pale gules and sable three lions passant per pale argent and or. Crest: A horse's head erased argent.

MacGrath: Quarterly: 1st, Argent three lions passant gules; 2nd, or a dexter hand lying fesswise couped at the wrist proper holding a cross formée fitchée azure; 3rd, Gules a dexter hand lying fesswise couped at the wrist proper holding a battle-axe erect or; 4th, Argent an antelope trippant sable attired or.

O'Griffy (Griffin): Sable a griffin segreant or langued and armed gules.

MacGuire: Vert a white horse fully caparisoned thereon a knight in full armour on his helmet a plume of ostrich feathers his right hand brandishing a sword all proper.

Gun: Argent three cannon barrels fesswise proper. Crest: A dexter hand couped at the wrist proper.

Hackett: Azure three hake fishes haurient in fess argent, on a chief of the second three shamrocks proper.

O'Hagan: Quarterly, argent and azure, 1st, a shoe proper, on a canton per chevron gules and ermine three covered cups or; 2nd, A flag of the first charged with a dexter hand of the fourth; 3rd A lion rampant of the sixth; 4th, A fish naient proper. Crest: A cubit arm proper vested gules cuffed ermine the hand grasping a dagger erect proper.

O'Halloran: Gules a horse passant argent saddled and bridled proper, on a chief of the second three mullets azure. Crest: A lizard or.

O'Hanlon: Vert on a mount in base proper a boar passant ermine. Crest: A lizard displayed vert.

O'Hanly: Vert a boar passant argent armed hoofed and crined or, between two arrows barways of the second headed of the third that in chief pointing to the dexter and that in base to the sinister.

O'Hannon: Quarterly gules and or, on a bend sable three crosses patée argent.

O'Hanraghty: Azure a griffin passant wings elevated or. Crest: on a helmet in profile visor closed a dolphin naiant all proper.

O'Hara: Vert on a pale radiant or a lion rampant sable.

O'Hart: Gules a lion passant guardant or, in base a human heart argent. Crest: A naked arm couped below the elbow and erect grasping a sword flammant all proper.

O'Hartagan: Azure a lion rampant or holding in each forepaw a dagger argent pommelled and hilted of the second. Crest: A gauntlet erect grasping a sword proper pommelled and hilted or.

Hatton: Azure on a chevron between three garbs or, an annulet gules. Crest: A hind statant or charged with an annulet as in the arms.

O'Hea: Argent a dexter arm lying fesswise couped below the elbow vested gules turned up of the first grasping in the hand a sword in pale entwined with a serpent descending all proper.

O'Heffernan: Per fess vert and gules, on a fess or a lion passant guardant azure, in chief three crescents or. Crest: A cubit arm erect in armour the hand gauntleted and holding a broken sword proper.

O'Hegarty: Argent an oak tree eradicated proper, on a chief gules three birds of the first beaked and legged sable. Crest: An arm in armour embowed the hand grasping a scymitar all proper.

O'Hennessy: Vert a stag trippant argent between six arrows two two and two saltirewise or. Crest: Between the attires of a stag fixed to the scalp or an arrow point downward gules headed and flighted or.

O'Heyne (Hynes): Per pale indented or and gules two lions rampant combatant counterchanged. Crest: A cubit arm armed embowed the hand grasping a sword all proper.

O'Hickey: Azure a lion passant guardant or, on a chief ermine a bend sable. Crest: A hand in a gauntlet erect holding a baton all proper.

O'Higgins: Argent gutée de poix on a fess sable three towers of the first. Crest: A tower sable issuant from the battlements a demi-griffin wings elevated argent holding in the dexter claw a sword proper.

O'Hogan: Sable on a chief or three annulets of the field.

O'Holohan: Azure a tower or supported by two lions rampant argent, in base two crescents of the last, on a chief of the third three annulets gules.

O'Horan: Vert three lions rampant two and one or. Crest: A demi-lion rampant or.

MacHugh: Argent a saltire vert between a dexter hand couped at the wrist in chief gules, two trefoils slipt of the second in fess and a boat with oars proper in base.

Hunt: Azure on a bend between two water bougets or three leopards" faces gules, and for augmentation, on a chief of the third a castle or port between two towers argent masoned sable with the Union Jack of England displayed from a flagstaff erect proper, and in a canton of the field an Irish harp of the second stringed of the fourth. Crest: A castle as in the arms.

O'Hurley: Argent on a gross gules five frets or.

MacInerney: Argent three lions passant in pale gules armed and langued azure. Crest: A mermaid proper.

Jebb: Quarterly: Vert and or, 1st, A falcon close argent belled of the second; 4th, A hawk's lure of the third.

Jordan (MacSurtain): Argent a fess sable, in base a lion passant of the last.

Joyce: Argent an eagle with two heads displayed gules, over-all a fess ermine. Crest: A demi-wolf argent ducally gorged or.

Kavanagh: Argent a lion passant gules, in base two crescents of the last. Crest: A crescent gules out of the horns thereof a garb or.

O'Keane (O'Cahan): Azure on a fess per pale gules and argent between in chief out of the horns of a crescent a dexter hand couped at the wrist and apaumée surmounted by an estoile between on the dexter a horse counter-salient and on the sinister a lion rampant each also surmounted by an estoile, and in base a salmon naiant all argent, on the dexter side three lizards passant in bend sinisterwise argent and on the sinister an oak tree eradicated vert, over all an escutcheon argent charged with a calvary cross on three grieces proper. Crest: A cat-a-mountain rampant proper.

Keane: Gules three salmon naiant in pile argent. Crest: A cat-a-mount sejeant guardant proper holding in the dexter forepaw a Union flag.

O'Kearney: Argent three lions rampant gules, on a chief azure between two phaeons of the first a gauntletted hand fesswise or holding a dagger erect proper pommelled and hilted or. Crest: A gauntleted hand holding a dagger as in the arms.

Keating: Argent a saltire gules between four nettle leaves vert. Crest: A boar statant gules armed and hoofed or holding in the mouth a nettle leaf vert.

O'Keefe: Vert a lion rampant or, in chief two dexter hands couped at the wrist erect and apaumée of the last. Crest: A griffin passant or holding in the dexter claw a sword proper.

Keith (Baroness, of Stonehaven Marischal, in the peerage of Ireland): Azure a chevron sable between three boars' heads erased gules. Supporters: Dexter, a savage proper wreathed head and middle with oak leaves vert, in his exterior hand a club resting on the right shoulder, on his breast a shield azure charged with three fleurs-de-lis or, at his feet an anchor sable; sinister, a stag proper attired and unguled or, collared azure the collar charged with three cinquefoils argent and pendent therefrom a shield of the last with a chief gules charged with three pallets or, the dexter hind foot resting on an anchor sable.

MacKenna: Vert a fess argent between three lions" heads affrontée or. Crest: A salmon naiant proper.

O'Kennedy: Sable three helmets in profile proper. An arm embowed vested azure holding a scymitar all proper.

Kennedy (Roderick): Per pale. Two lions rampant combatant. Tinctures unknown. See main text.

Kennedy (President John Fitzgerald): Sable three helmets in profile or, within a border per saltire gules and ermine. Crest: Between two olive branches a cubit sinister arm in armour erect, the hand holding a sheaf of four arrows points upward all proper.

MacKeogh: Argent a lion rampant gules, in the dexter chief a dexter hand couped at the wrist and in the sinister a crescent both of the second. Crest a boar passant azure.

MacKeown: Argent two lions rampant combatant sable supporting a dexter hand couped at the wrist gules, in chief four mullets, of eight points gules, in base waves of the sea therein a salmon naiant all proper. Crest: An arm embowed in chain armour the hand holding a sword blade wavy all proper.

O'Kieran: Vert on a chevron argent three leopards' faces gules. Crest: A demi-lion rampant sable holding in the dexter paw a sword erect proper hilted and pommelled or.

O'Kinneally: Gules a stag statant argent.

Kinsella: Argent a fess gules between the chief two garbs of the last and in base a lion passant sable.

Kinsellagh: Vert two lions rampant combatant or, armed and langued gules on a chief quarterly of the second and sable an eft passant proper. Crest: A demi-eft salient proper.

O'Kirwan: Argent a chevron sable between three Cornish choughs proper. Crest: A Cornish chough proper.

De Lacy (Lacy): Or a lion rampant purpure.

Lally (O'Mullally): Argent three eagles displayed gules two and one each holding in the beak a sprig of laurel proper between as many crescents one and two azure. Crest: An eagle as in the arms.

O'Lalor: Or a lion rampant guardant gules.

O'Leary: Argent a lion passant in base gules, in chief a ship of three masts sable sails set proper from the stern the flag of St George flotant. Crest: Out of a ducal coronet or an arm in armour embowed holding a sword proper pommelled and hilted or.

O'Lonergan: Argent on a chevron azure three estoiles or, in chief two arrows in saltire points downwards gules. Crest: An arrow in pale point downward distilling drops of blood all proper.

O'Loughlin: Gules a man in complete armour facing the sinister shooting an arrow from a bow all proper. Crest: An anchor entwined with a cable proper.

MacLoughlin (O'Melaghlin): Per fess, the chief two coats: 1st, argent three dexter hands couped at the wrist two and one gules; 2nd, A lion rampant gules armed and langued azure; the base barry wavy azure and argent a salmon naiant proper.

MacLoughlin (Tirconnell): Per fess azure and gules, in chief a lion rampant or between two swords erect argent pommelled and hilted or, in base three crescents argent.

Lynch: Azure a chevron between three trefoils slipt or. Crest: A lynx passant azure collared or.

MacLysaght: Argent three spears erect in fess gules, on a chief azure a lion passant guardant or. Crest: Issuant from clouds a naked arm bent holding a short sword by the blade all proper.

O'Madden: Sable a falcon trussing a mallard argent.

MacMahon (Oriel): Argent an ostrich sable holding in the beak a horseshoe or. Crest: A naked arm embowed holding a sword all proper the point pierced through a fleur-de-lis sable.

MacMahon (Thomond): Argent three lions passant reguardant in pale gules armed and langued azure. Crest: A dexter arm in armour embowed proper garnished or holding in the hand a sword both proper pommel and hilt or.

O'Mahoney: Quarterly: 1st and 4th, Or a lion rampant azure; 2nd, per pale argent and gules a lion rampant counterchange; 3rd, Argent a chevron gules between three snakes tongued proper. Crest: Out of a viscount's coronet or an arm in armour embowed holding a sword proper pommelled and hilted or pierced through a fleur-de-lis azure.

O'Malley: Or a boar passant gules. Crest: A ship with three masts sails set all proper.

O'Malone: Vert a lion rampant or between three mullets argent. Crest: A man in full armour in the dexter hand a spear resting on the ground all proper.

Mangan: Sable a dexter hand apaumée argent between in chief two annulets and in base a crescent or. Crest: A dexter hand apaumée sable charged with an annulet or.

MacManus: Vert a griffin segreant or, in chief three crescents argent. Crest: A dexter arm couped below the elbow erect holding a long cross proper.

Martin: Azure a cross calvary on three grieces argent, the dexter arm terminating in a sun in splendour or, the sinister in a decrescent argent. Crest: an estoile or.

O'Meagher: Azure two lions rampant combatant or supporting a sword argent pommelled and hilted of the second, in base two crescents of the third. Crest: A falcon argent belled or.

O'Meara: Gules three lions passant gardant in pale per pale or and argent, a border azure charged with eight escallops argent. Crest: A pelican vulning herself proper.

O'Meehan: Gules on a chevron argent three bucks' heads erased of the field attired or, in base a demi-lion rampant of the second. Crest: A griffin's head erased wings endorsed or.

Molyneaux (Daniel, Ulster King of Arms, 1597): Azure, a cross moline or quarter pierced of the field, in dexter chief a fleur-de-lis of the second. Crest: An heraldic tyger passant argent holding in the dexter forepaw a cross moline or.

O'Molloy: Argent a lion rampant sable between three trefoils slipt gules. Crest: In front of an oak tree growing out of a mount all proper a greyhound springing sable collared or.

O'Molony: Azure, on the dexter side a quiver of three arrows, on the sinister a bow erect all or.

O'Monahan: Azure a chevron between three mullets or. Crest: A knight in complete armour resting the sinister hand upon the hip and holding in the dexter a tilting spear thereon a forked pennon charged with an escutcheon of arms.

O'Mooney: Argent a holly tree eradicated vert thereon a lizard passant or, a border compony counter-compony of the field and second.

O'Moran: Sable three stars of six points rayed or. Crest: A star of six points rayed or.

O'More: Vert a lion rampant or, in chief three mullets of the last. Crest: A dexter hand fesswise couped at the wrist holding a sword in pale pierced through three gory heads all proper.

O'Moriarty: Argent an eagle displayed sable. Crest: An arm in armour embowed holding a sword fesswise entwined with a snake all proper.

O'Moroney: Azure a chevron or between three boars' heads couped argent langued gules. Crest: A boar's head couped argent.

Morris: Or a fess dancetée sable in base a lion rampant of the second. Crest: A lion's head erased argent gutée de sang.

O'Mulally (Lally): (See above)

O'Mullan: Argent a dexter hand couped at the wrist in fess gules holding a dagger in pale proper between three crescents gules. Crest: Out of a crescent gules a dagger erect proper.

Mullins (de Moleyns, Lord Ventry): Azure a cross moline or quarter pierced of the field at the dexter chief point a crescent of the second. Crest: A Saracen's head afrontée couped below the shoulders proper.

O'Mulvihil: Per fess argent and gules, in chief two lions rampant combatant azure supporting a dexter hand couped at the wrist gules and in base a salmon naiant proper; in base an Irish harp or stringed argent between two battle axes in pale the blades turned outwards proper.

O'Murphy (Muskerry): Quarterly argent and gules, on a fess sable between four lions rampant counterchanged three garbs or.

O'Morchoe (Murphy): Argent an apple tree eradicated fructed proper, on a chief vert a lion passant or. Crest: On a chapeau gules turned up ermine a lion rampant of the first holding between the paws a garb or.

MacMorrogh: Gules a lion rampant argent.

Nagle: Ermine on a fess azure three losenges or. Crest: A nightingale or.

MacNally: Gules an arm in armour proper garnished or embowed couped at the shoulder holding in the hand a battle-axe of the second between six martlets argent three and three palewise, at the centre chief point an ancient Irish crown. Crest: A naked cubit arm couped erect proper holding a dagger of the first pommelled and hilted or.

MacNamara: Gules a lion rampant argent, in chief two spearheads or.

O'Neilan: Sable two unicorns passant in pale argent horned and hoofed or. Crest: A dexter hand erect couped at the wrist grasping a dagger all proper.

O'Neill: Argent two lions rampant combatant supporting a dexter hand apaumée couped at the wrist all gules, in chief three estoiles of the second, in base three waves of the sea therein a salmon naiant all proper. See text.

O'Nolan: Argent on a cross gules a lion passant between four martlets of the first, in each quarter a sword erect of the second. Crest: A martlet argent.

Nugent (Ancient): Ermine two bars gules.

Nugent (Earl of Westmeath and Baron Devlin): Quarterly: 1st, Nugent; 2nd, Fitzjohn: quarterly, or and gules a bordure vair; 3rd, Drake, argent a wyvern tail nowed gules; 4th, Argent a chevron sable between three doors close azure; 5th, Gules seven mascles conjoined, three, three and one or; 6th, or a fret gules. Crest: A cockatrice wings elevated vert, tail nowed, combed and wattled gules. Supporters: Two cockatrices, wings elevated and endorsed vert, tails nowed, combed and wattled gules.

Ottley: Argent, on a fess azure three garbs or.

O'Phelan: Argent four losenges in bend conjoined azure between two cottises of the last, on a chief gules three fleur-de-lis of the field. Crest: A stag's head or.

Plunkett: Sable a bend argent, in the sinister chief a tower triple-towered of the second. Crest: A horse passant argent.

Power: Argent a chief indented sable.

Purcell: Or a saltire between four boar's heads couped sable. Crest: A cubit arm erect habited azure cuffed argent grasping in the hand proper a sword of the last pommelled and hilted or.

O'Quigley: Gules an orle argent over all a bend erminois. Crest: An estoile argent.

MacQuillan: Gules a wolf rampant argent, a chief or. A demi-dragon azure.

O'Quin (Annaly): Vert a pegasus passant wings elevated argent, a chief or.

O'Quin (Thomond): Gules a hand couped below the

wrist grasping a sword all proper between in chief two crescents argent and in base as many serpents erect respectant tails nowed or.

O'Quinlan: Per pale ermine and or two lions rampant combatant between in chief a mullet surmounted of a crescent and in base a dexter hand couped at the wrist and erect all gules.

O'Rafferty: Ermine an eagle displayed sable, over all a fess or charged with two salmon naiant gules. Crest: On a mount vert an eagle displayed or.

Redmond: Gules a castle bi-turreted argent between three woolpacks or. Crest: A beacon fired proper.

O'Regan: Or a chevron ermine between three dolphins azure.

O'Reilly: Vert two lions rampant combatatant or supporting a dexter hand apaumée couped at the wrist bloody all proper.

Reynolds (MacRannall): Vert a lion rampant between three escallops or. Crest: On a mount a stag couchant proper.

Rice: Quarterly: 1st and 4th, per pale indented gules and argent, 2nd and 3rd, azure a lion rampant of the second. On an inescutcheon the arms of Spring, Or, on a chevron gules three cinquefoils argent between three mascles sable. Crest: A leopard's face ducally crowned.

O'Riordan: Quarterly: 1st and 4th, Gules out of clouds in the sinister side a dexter arm fesswise proper holding a dagger in pale argent pommelled and hilted or. 2nd and 3rd, Argent a lion rampant gules against a tree in the dexter couped proper. Crest: A fleur-de-lis gules.

Roche: Gules three roaches naiant in pale. Crest: On a rock proper an osprey rising argent beaked and legged or holding in the claws a roach of the second.

O'Rourke: Or two lions passant in pale sable. Crest: Out of an antique Irish crown or an arm in armour erect grasping a sword proper pommelled and hilted of the first.

Ryan (O'Mulrian): Gules three griffins' heads erased argent. Crest: A griffin segreant gules holding in the sinister claw a dagger proper.

Sarsfield: Per pale argent and gules a fleur-de-lis counterchanged.

O'Scanlan: Per fess indented argent and azure three lions rampant counterchanged.

Seymour: Gules two wings conjoined in lure argent.

MacShanly: Azure a lion passant or, in chief three estoiles of the last.

O'Shaughnessy: Vert two lions rampant combatant or supporting a tower triple towered argent. Crest: An arm embowed the hand grasping a spear point downward all proper.

O'Shea: Per bend azure and or two fleur-de-lis counterchanged.

O'Sheehan: Azure on a mount in base vert a dove argent holding in the beak an olive branch proper. Crest: A dove as in the arms.

MacSheehy: Quarterly: 1st, azure a lion passant gardant argent; 2nd, Argent three lizards vert; 3rd, azure three pole-axes in fess or; 4th, Argent a ship with three masts sable. Crest: An arm in armour couped below the elbow erect holding in the hand a sword blade entwined with a serpent all proper.

O'Sheridan: Or a lion rampant between three trefoils vert. Crest: Out of a ducal coronet or a stag's head proper.

O'Shiel: Argent a lion rampant between two dexter hands couped at the wrist erect apaumée in chief and a mullet in base all gules. Crest: Out of a ducal coronet or an arm erect vested gules holding a sword proper.

Sneyd: Argent a scythe the blade in chief, the handle in bend sinister on the fess point a fleur-de-lis both sable. Crest: A lion passant gardant sable.

Spring: See Rice.

O'Sullivan Mor: Per fess, the base per pale, in chief or a dexter hand couped at the wrist gules grasping a sword erect entwined with a serpent proper between two lions rampant respectant of the second, on the dexter base vert a stag trippant or, on the sinister base per pale argent and sable a boar passant counterchanged. Crest: On a ducal coronet or a robin redbreast holding in the beak a sprig of laurel all proper.

O'Sullivan Beare: Per pale argent and sable, a fess between in chief a boar passant all counterchanged armed hoofed and crined or. Crest: On a lizard vert a robin redbreast proper.

MacSweeny: Or on a fess vert between three boars passant sable a lizard argent. Crest: An arm in armour embowed holding a battle-axe all proper.

Taafe: Gules a cross argent fretty azure. Crest: An arm in armour embowed holding in the hand a sword all proper pommelled and hilted or.

MacTiernan: Ermine two lions passant gules. Crest: A griffin statant gules wings erect vert.

O'Tierney: Argent a chevron sable, a chief gules. Crest: An oak tree proper.

Tobin: Azure three oak leaves argent.

O'Toole: Gules a lion passant proper. Crest: A boar passant proper.

O'Trehy (Troy): Azure two griffins segreant combatant or. Crest: A tiger's head erased or.

Tully (MacAtilla): Vert a chevron between three wolves' heads erased argent. Crest: A wolf's head couped argent.

de Vere (Robert, Duke of Ireland, Marquess of Dublin, Earl of Oxford): Quarterly: 1st and 4th, by patent 9 of Richard II Azure, three crowns or, a bordure argent; 2nd and 3rd, Vere, quarterly: gules and or, in the first quarter a mullet argent.

Vernon: Argent a fret sable. Crest: A boar's head erased sable ducally gorged.

Wall: Azure a lion rampant between three crosses crosslet or. Crest: A naked arm embowed holding a scymitar the blade gutée de sang all proper.

Walsh: Argent a chevron gules between three broad arrowheads sable. Crest: A swan pierced through the back and breast with a dart all proper.

Woulfe: Per fess argent and azure, in chief on a mount vert in front of an oak tree a wolf passant both proper, in base two salmon naiant barways in pale argent. Crest: A stork wings elevated sable.